Finding the Path Home
A Story of Trust and Perseverance

Carline Samuels

TEACH Services, Inc.
PUBLISHING
www.TEACHServices.com • (800) 367-1844

World rights reserved. This book or any portion thereof may not be copied or reproduced in any form or manner whatever, except as provided by law, without the written permission of the publisher, except by a reviewer who may quote brief passages in a review.

The author assumes full responsibility for the accuracy of all facts and quotations as cited in this book. The opinions expressed in this book are the author's personal views and interpretations, and do not necessarily reflect those of the publisher.

This book is provided with the understanding that the publisher is not engaged in giving spiritual, legal, medical, or other professional advice. If authoritative advice is needed, the reader should seek the counsel of a competent professional.

The author assumes full responsibility for the accuracy and interpretation of the Ellen White quotations cited in this book.

Copyright © 2022 Carline Samuels
Copyright © 2022 TEACH Services, Inc.
ISBN-13: 978-1-4796-1416-5 (Paperback)
ISBN-13: 978-1-4796-1417-2 (ePub)
Library of Congress Control Number: 2022910051

All scripture quotations, unless otherwise indicated, are taken from the King James Version.

Scripture quotations marked NKJV are taken from the New King James Version®. Copyright © 1982 by Thomas Nelson. Used by permission. All rights reserved.

Published by

www.TEACHServices.com • (800) 367-1844

Table of Contents

Acknowledgements v
Introduction vii

1. The Sad News 9
2. The Sabbath 14
3. The Newscast 16
4. The Decision 17
5. The Wait 25
6. Off We Go 27
7. The Journey to Halls Delight 29
8. At the Funeral 32
9. At the Graveside 34
10. On and Off 36
11. Overnighting 40

12. Morning at Halls Delight....................................42
13. Departure from Halls Delight..............................45
14. The Climb..51
15. From the Rock to the Bridge 56
16. The Prayer...60
17. Rivers and Mountains—Our Separation from God........68
18. Square at Last...72
19. Leaving Mavis Bank...73
20. Angels—Our Special Silent Guides 78
21. In One Accord 80
22. Home Here We Come.....................................83
23. Home in View..87
24. Revival and Reformation.................................104
25. Keep Pressing On..107
26. Home at Last 111
    About the Author..117
    References 118

Acknowledgements

I want to thank everyone who played a part so that I was able to compile this story. To my co-workers, Merlyn Walker, Veneice Bryan, and Hirfa Minto, for making this happen. To Pastor Willis and his wife and the Adventist group from Trelawny, Jamaica. To the people who assisted us one way or another, helping us crossing the river and getting us to our car. To all those who assisted us from Mavis Bank Square to Kingston. To all the people who have read this book and given me their comments—my co-workers at the North Jamaica Conference of SDA, my freshman composition teacher at Northern Caribbean University, Brown's Town extension, and my friend Marlene Golding. Last, but not least, special thanks to my husband Holness and children (Kathrina, Shani, Kara, and Kevaun), my mother Evelyn, and my siblings Bedel, Unet, Paul, Daniel, and Aletha, who have always supported me in my writing.

Thank You

Introduction

This is a true story about a group of Christians who attended a funeral service for the mother of one of their staff members in the hills of St. Andrew, Jamaica. The island was experiencing terrible weather conditions during the period, and the group braved the weather and ventured out on the trip to the funeral.

The group experienced life-threatening experiences, going to and from the funeral service. These testimonies have been captured and presented in story form—titled "Finding the Path Home." In this book you will see how God protected His children through trying situations such as the ones that the group experienced. You will understand how these workers had to cross rivers and climbed mountains to get home. Through this terrible ordeal, you will also come to the realization that our God is still in control and is able to offer protection and guidance in any situation.

In our spiritual journey, readers will be encouraged to hold on to God's unchanging hands as we are nearing our heavenly home. Like the trials we went through trying to go to our physical homes, we have many tribulations and obstacles in our Christian walk. It is the author's intention to link going home from the funeral service to going to our heavenly home. It will compare the obstacles that Satan puts in our paths and show how God works individually and collectively to help us overcome those obstacles. It is the hope that reading this book will serve to comfort, encourage, and guide our readers to place total dependence on God through their spiritual journey. The author's aim is to get readers who feel like they want to give up the Christian walk to be encouraged to press on, and those who have not yet found Jesus Christ may be led to Him through these true-to-life testimonies and encouragements.

Heavenly Father, please be with the readers of this book, touch hearts and minds, and help that they will not be distracted by the devil because we know that he is working cunningly right now to distract minds and to cause people to lose interest. In the name of Jesus Christ, I claim victory over all problems for all those who will attempt to read this book, and at the end, the decision to serve God wholeheartedly will be made.

Chapter 1

The Sad News

It was Thursday morning, October 13, 2005, and the day at the office started out like any other day. North Jamaica Mission is located in the garden parish of St. Ann, Jamaica, and is positioned off the St. Ann's Bay main road leading to Ocho Rios. The office is sited on hilly terrain and away from the hustle and bustle of the town of St. Ann's Bay. The daily morning devotions that started at 8:00 a.m. were already completed, and this set the pace for working in an environment where the Spirit of God was felt and lingered throughout the day. The very soft background gospel music penetrated the silence in the office and gave it a heavenly atmosphere. The end of the workweek was fast approaching, and there was a lot of work to be done before mid-day on Friday. Workers were therefore busy at their desks or in their offices attending to their jobs. The atmosphere was quite peaceful, and sometimes, melodious voices could be heard singing along with the songs that were being played throughout the entire office. It was just a blessing to be at work each day because of the very good staff rapport and spiritual connection at the office.

North Jamaica Mission, now known as North Jamaica Conference of Seventh-day Adventists (NJC), was an exceptional place to work. I resigned from my job as administrative assistant to the general manager of a prominent five-star hotel in Trelawny, Jamaica, and assumed responsibilities of receptionist at the conference office. Yes, I accepted a demotion because I gave up all the benefits and far better working conditions to work at the North Jamaica Conference. I was also receiving a lesser pay at the office, but I was doing much more work. I gave up all this to have a peace of mind and to be more spiritually connected with the

Lord. At NJC, I was later promoted to cashier and departmental secretary and finally, administrative assistant to the president, secretary, and treasurer.

I started working at the conference office just a few months after it was opened in 2002, so the working conditions were less than ideal. The offices were not completely renovated, and the equipment and fixtures were not fully installed. There was just one phone with no extensions, and this made it impossible to transfer telephone calls. Considering this, I would constantly be on my feet, trying to let people know that there was a call for them. Where I was coming from, there were approximately four telephone operators working at any one time handling incoming and outgoing calls. The treasury office was the main office at the time, and several people had to work around one large desk. Coming from a fully air-conditioned office to one where there was none, made the heat more unbearable at times to withstand. I, however, purposed in my heart that I would give this job my best, as I was now working for the Lord. I gave God my promise that if He gave me a job at the NJC, I would perform my task to the very best at all times. I worked hard at my previous jobs, and there was no doubt that I was going to do the same at NJC. The poem below was a promise I made to God after I started working at the conference that I would do my best.

My New Job

I waited very, very long, and then suddenly the time was here.
To attend for an interview, this brought such great fear.
But I got myself together and went to North Jamaica Mission.
I know that with the help of God, I would overcome any situation.

So, finally, at Bruco, I handed my resignation.
They could not understand why I was leaving such very good job condition.
But I knew it was time, for many times I would pray.
For God to help me leave Bruco, and I knew He would make a way.

Chapter 1: The Sad News

North Jamaica Mission—a place different from where I was leaving.
Worship in the mornings! It makes the entire day a blessing.
The staff members are easy to work with; they are children of God.
Thank You, Jesus, for removing me from the environment that I thought was so bad!

I am now able to work hard to help touch so many, many lives.
I pray and ask God to help me; without Him, I just cannot survive.
I put my trust and faith in God, for He will lead me aright.
With God's leading and directing, there is no need for fright.

The hard work done at Lido Bruco was to the best of my ability.
And the hard work at North Jamaica Mission is the same reality.
So, I am making a pledge to continue working hard each and every day,
For I know when Jesus comes, my reward He will surely pay.

By: Carline Samuels

Even though there were many challenges initially, it was a great pleasure working for the Lord. I was graciously welcomed, and in no time, I was getting close to the workers in the office and to the pastors. The office consisted of a president, secretary, treasurer, auditor, administrative assistant, receptionist, office attendant, accountants, departmental directors, and more than twenty pastors, who were stationed in more than one hundred and thirty churches in the parishes of Trelawny, St. Ann, and St. Mary. Later, the office served and is still serving churches in the parishes of St. Ann and Trelawny.

Hirfa Minto and Veneice Bryan joined the staff at NJC months after I was employed there. Hirfa was employed as a receptionist, and I was promoted to cashier and departmental secretary. Hirfa was hardworking, and she got on amicably with all the workers. She could be described as a prayer warrior, and she used her breaks at lunchtime to pray for others and herself and family. Veneice Bryan was more on the quiet side, but she also displayed good Christian qualities. She is a teacher by profession but was employed at the conference to assist with a life insurance plan for members.

Merlyn Walker later joined the conference as the IML manager (a financial investment scheme for the union conference. Both NJC and IML were under the West Indies Union Conference of Seventh-day Adventists. This union was later split, and we now have the Jamaica Union Conference of Seventh-day Adventists. Merlyn is a very gracious woman who has a warm and pleasant personality. She is serious about working for the Lord, and she will go more than the extra mile to help someone in need.

Pastor Willis was one of the pastors who loved to pray. He would visit the office frequently for meetings, and we would have very uplifting conversations with him. He is a very dedicated worker and a committed Christian. He is kind-hearted and always tries to reflect Christ in every way possible. His beautiful wife and two sons played an integral part in his ministry. One could not meet Pastor Willis and not love him.

It was, therefore, a very sad Thursday morning when we heard about the passing of Pastor Willis' mother. After much deliberation as to whether or not we should attend the funeral service (because of continuous rain for over a week), Merlyn, Minto, Veneice, and I decided that we would attend. This would be held on Sunday, October 16, 2005. I did not know exactly where we were going, only that we were going to Mavis Bank, St. Andrew. We decided to go even though the entire island of Jamaica was experiencing bad inclement weather.

I left work at noon on Friday, did my shopping, and then went home to prepare for the Sabbath. Dinner was very lovely. We had split pea soup, and I also looked after steamed callaloo for breakfast for Sabbath morning. Preparation is normally done before, as no cooking is done on the Sabbath. Devotions are normally very spirit-filled on Friday evenings, as our doors at home were always open, welcoming our church members who want to join us for vesper services. Sometimes, we would also visit other members to have vesper services at their homes. The beautiful voices would blend to give God thanks and praise in songs, testimonies, and prayers for taking us safely through another week and allowing us to see another Sabbath evening. Sometimes passersby would stand by just to listen to our beautiful singing. On this particular night, it was raining, so we had a very short devotion, and soon, we were in bed.

Chapter 2

The Sabbath

It was a wet Sabbath morning, but, as usual, my family and I got up early, and very soon, we had our breakfast and were in church having a wonderful time.

That Sabbath was Children's Day and the continuous rain did not prevent church members from attending church and supporting the children's program. The children were in charge of every aspect of the church service; therefore, they started off with song service at 9:15 a.m., they conducted Sabbath School, divine worship service, and also AYS (a program for the young people, which takes place in the evening one hour before sunset). I was in charge of the Children's Choir, and they did exceptionally well. There were four child speakers, and each had a unique presentation, and through the working and leading of the Holy Spirit, delivered timely and soul-searching messages. My then 12-year-old daughter, Kathrina, was the moderator in the divine service, and she also played the keyboard. The theme for the day was "Shine for Jesus." Even though it rained, the children really shone for Jesus, and though it was raining on the outside, tears of joy were raining in our hearts.

At the end of the service, we all scattered and went our separate ways. While standing in front of my house, Vana, a church member, who was passing by in her car, shouted out to us that "Wilma" was on her way. Wilma? Which Wilma? Are we going to get a hurricane? Jamaica is a tropical island, and each year we are hammered with a lot of tropical depressions, cold fronts, and hurricane threats, and hurricanes during the hurricane season. I remembered one year we got a hurricane, and before the week was ended, we were bracing for another one. Was Wilma a disaster waiting to happen? Why would she want to visit us on such short

Chapter 2: The Sabbath 15

notice? Would Wilma prevent us from going to the funeral service the next day? We did not know of any weather system that was developing by that name, and this made it unclear to us why Vana made that statement. Also, we did not get any weather report later on in the evening that justified Vana's comment. We, therefore, dismissed the idea that we were getting another storm.

I would normally do my laundry on Saturday nights, but seeing that the coming Monday would have been Heroes Day, which was a public holiday in Jamaica, I opted not to, as the washing could be done on Heroes Day. Seeing that I had a long journey ahead of me the next day, very soon, I was getting ready for bed.

Chapter 3

The Newscast

At that time, there were only two local television stations in Jamaica, and many people who did not have cable or Dish Network available to them would have only these two channels at their disposal. We were viewing one of such channels, the CVM 8:00 p.m. newscast, when I realized that the roads to Mavis Bank were blocked. I remembered that we should be in that area for the funeral service the next day, so I got a little concerned. I wanted to call Merlyn to find out what was happening, but my phone needed charging. When I got home, I put the phone on charge, and as soon as I was able to power it on, the phone rang. Merlyn's concerned and questionable voice met mine, and we started to talk about what the blockage at Mavis Bank meant and if this would prevent us from going to the funeral as planned.

> **We realized that it would be very dangerous to travel in that area.**

We did not know the Mavis Bank community, but by looking at what was taking place there, we realized that it would be very dangerous to travel in that area. Water was everywhere; gullies were flooded out; the roads were flooded out as well; rivers were overflowing their banks, and there were landslides in some areas. In other areas roads were impassable due to the high volume of water that enveloped them, turning into lakes. With this new information, we decided that we would not go to the funeral.

Chapter 4

The Decision

My husband and I decided to do the laundry after all on Saturday night. We had a washing machine but not a dryer. It would be a waste to have a dryer as in Jamaica, most days are sunny. However, when it does rain, I would have loved to have a dryer as sometimes it can rain up to two weeks without getting any break. That Sunday morning was one of those times when I wished I had a dryer.

Even though it was cold and wet, there were just very fine droplets of rain, and because it was breezy, I got up a bit earlier on Sunday morning trying to hang the clothes out, hoping that the breeze would get some of the water out of the clothes before the rains came again. There were clothes that were needed for Monday morning, such as uniforms for the children to wear to school. The school system in Jamaica requires that students be properly uniformed at all times while at school.

While I was on the third line, Kathrina brought the phone to me. Merlyn had decided that she was going to the funeral. I told her that she should have called me earlier and that I did not think I would be able to make it. I told her that when she was passing by my bus stop, if she did not see me, then she should go right ahead. We were supposed to leave at 8:00 a.m. for a 2:30 p.m. funeral service. However, my husband said that if Merlyn was willing to wait a little later, I could go in support of my colleague in his time of bereavement. I called Merlyn and told her that if she was willing to pick me up at 9:00 a.m., then I would go to the funeral.

We were all dressed for the funeral, and even though we left so early in the morning, none of us took any extra clothing. All I had was a pair of open-toe slippers. The others also had an extra pair of flat shoes.

Before making the decision to go to the funeral, many times, our minds were influenced negatively, and even after we made the decision to go, we had many doubts. This was all due to the continuous bad weather. We heard about landslides, flooding in some areas, and other negative incidents that related to the bad weather. Yes, we wanted to go and support Pastor Willis, but we were also scared for our lives as we did not know what lay ahead.

How many times have we tried to make decisions for God, but the devil put things in our path to sidetrack us? When he does this, we become fearful and doubtful, and soon, we ignore the biddings of the Holy Spirit and turn away from our convictions. Satan presents all our sins before us and makes us feel guilty. He tells us that we are worthless, and God will not hear us and forgive us our sins. We then start to think of all the terrible things we have done, and because to us it seemed insurmountable, we believe that it is impossible for us to change. He shows us how impossible it will be to follow Christ, and we continue to allow the storms of life to ravage us and break us down, causing a flood of sin and sorrow to envelop our paths. As a result, we continue to live in sin and shame.

Chapter 4: The Decision

Before I accepted the Advent message, I accompanied my fiancé to an evangelistic meeting that the Adventist group was having in my area. I decided that I would just visit one night. I always looked at Adventists as some weird people who do some really strange things that were not necessarily required of God. I looked at their religious practices as outdated and more of a legalistic approach to worship. I was very eager to let my fiancé know that any day is a good day to choose for the Sabbath. Any day could be chosen for the day of worship. My husband at the time was not a practicing Adventist, but he was convicted about the issue of the Sabbath.

I attended this meeting with skepticism, and I sat all the way in the back, hoping that it would be over soon. The preacher was preaching on the topic of the Sabbath, and I was surprised to hear the points that he was making concerning the Sabbath. To top it off, he was backing up all his points with scriptures from the Bible. Some of these scriptures I did not know were in the Bible. I was convicted that very night on the issue of the Sabbath, but I said nothing to my fiancé.

Satan then started to put all sorts of things before me. If you accept the Sabbath, you will have to give up this, and you will have to give up that. I told myself that I would visit the church sometimes and go to my regular church at other times. I, therefore, started attending the Adventist church, and soon after, I started going every Sabbath. I was, however, still doing my business on the Sabbath because I thought it was impossible to have it done any other day of the week.

My fiancé and I later decided to get married. I still wanted my first-day pastor to be a part of the wedding, so we decided to let him conduct the ceremony but on a Sunday. We had it all planned. But because God has everything in control, and when we believe we have made our plans and they are cast in concrete, God uproots those plans. My Sunday pastor was not able to do the wedding on that particular day; therefore, the Adventist pastor performed our wedding, and it was beautiful. We later got baptized in 2000 and immediately got actively involved in church activities.

The song below was my first song that I wrote shortly after I made the decision to follow Christ all the way.

Give me a New Heart

Jesus, I know I have sinned and come short of Thy glory.
Give me a new heart; let me go and tell Your story,
How you died on the cross so that men might live.
Help me be a witness that mine enemies I'll forgive

Chorus
Give me a new heart, dear Lord, I pray
Give me a new heart as I go along life's way
Let me tell of Your story, how You died on the cross
So that all men, all men might live.

Jesus, I will surely tell of Your name to both far and near
How You comfort me when I am in despair.
O, Lord, there is none, there is no one like You
Help me be a witness, a true witness for You.

Dear Lord, I thank You for giving to me a new heart;
My knowledge of You to others I'll impart.
I am now rejoicing; I'll praise You each day
For revealing to me the true and holy way.
By: Carline Samuels

Before I got baptized, I was attending a Certified Professional Secretary's (CPS) course, and this was only held on Sabbaths. This course was very expensive, and if I were successful, my job would have reimbursed me all the money I paid for it. I was, therefore, working very hard because not only did I want to become a Certified Professional Secretary, but I wanted the money as well. This became an issue before and after I was baptized because classes were only held on Sabbaths. I decided that I would go to church some Sabbaths and go to classes the other Sabbaths. The first Sabbath I went to church after I was baptized, I decided that I would not go back to classes on Sabbaths. How would I get through this? How would I pass the course? After we were baptized, the church hosted in a six-week crusade. I became involved in this, and we attended the meetings every night for the six weeks. I was working a nine-to-five job and was attending these meetings. There was no time for study.

What was I going to do? I know that God is interested in not only the spiritual, but He wants us to be successful in all our endeavors. In 3 John 2, John says, "Beloved, I wish above all things that thou mayest prosper and be in health, even as thy soul prospereth." Christ said that we should occupy until He comes. I put the situation before Christ, and I knew He would have made a way out for me.

I explained the situation to my friends who were also attending the classes, and we decided to form a study group. We would meet once or twice per week after work, and we would discuss what was taught the previous Sabbath. Sometimes I was so confused, and it seemed I was totally lost and had no way of managing the exams. I would often pray and ask the Lord to help me through this. I reminded Him that I made the decision to follow Him, and I was now seeking His help in order to be successful.

I remember one evening I was ridiculed by my friends. One of my friends, in particular, told me that I needed to attend classes, and God will understand if I did. Well, I stood firm on my faith and the promise I made to God. I continued going to church. I took the exam, and, praise the Lord, I was successful in all areas. I became a certified professional secretary. The person who ridiculed me the most failed the exam, even though she attended all the Saturday classes and study groups.

When we make decisions for Christ, He will see us through any situation the devil will throw at us. When I made that decision, so many questions came upon me. When will I do this, or when will I do that? Now, I look back and realize that Satan was just planting doubts in my mind. Today, he still does the same thing. I realize today that on a Sabbath, I do not want to be any place other than in the house of the Lord.

I encourage you to make the decision for Christ. It might be hard because you might believe you are going to lose your job, your family. It just might not be the case, and if you do, God will provide for you. He is in control of everything. Just make the decision and hold God to His promises. The three Hebrew boys determined in their hearts not to bow down to Nebuchadnezzar's image. And they also proclaimed that even if God did not rescue them from the fiery furnace, they would not bow to the image. God came through for them and rescued them from the fire.

Once we make that decision to follow Christ, we must let go and let God. Let go and let God unloose our shackles, let go and let God work out our job situation, let go and let God work out our school situation, let go and let God work on our families, friends, and our marriages. Let go and let God direct our path, even our path to the funeral service.

I remember another time when I was working at a particular place, I had to attend a Profit and Loss Review meeting each quarter to take the minutes. These meetings normally start at about 9:00 a.m. and would go up until about 4:00 or sometimes 5:00 p.m. We would be in this room, and lunch and any other food needed would be served from there. It was always a very tedious meeting.

In the month of December, the owners would have two meetings from different properties. The normally one-day meeting is then pressed for half a day, making it more challenging. One particular time, two meetings were for a Friday. To make matters worse, the meeting that I should attend was set not for a Friday morning but a Friday afternoon. I prayed and asked the Lord to have His way. I did my part of the work with due diligence. I did not complain or ask why the meeting was set at that time because they knew I was an Adventist. I did my reports and had everything that I needed to set up. I continued praying while I was preparing for the meeting. I purposed in my heart that I would not go beyond 5:00 p.m. The issue was that sun sets earlier in the month of December, and this would infringe on Sabbath time. I decided that politely I would ask to be excused when the time comes. I anticipated that the meeting would go well in the night, and I knew I was not going to stay, so I continued to pray. How would I get up and tell the owners and other top executives that I was

Chapter 4: The Decision

leaving? I did not know, but I purposed in my heart to do so, and I asked God for strength, determination, and willpower.

It was very strange that the day for the meeting came and went without anybody showing up. No one called or sent in their apologies for absences. We heard that some people were even in the US attending to other companies' businesses. This had never happened before, and neither did it ever happened in the future for the remainder of the time that I worked for that company. While the managers where I worked were surprised about the situation, I was giving God thanks and praise for His divine intervention and deliverance in that matter.

Let us make decisions for Christ because when we do so, He will stand for us. Let us stand for Him and trust Him to bring about favorable outcomes. We do not know why He allows certain things to happen when we stand for Him but let us trust God on all issues. I was telling myself that today I was going to lose my job. I was wondering what I was going to do. I had bills to pay, but while I was saying, "Today I will be jobless," Christ was saying, "Today you will have experienced another victory!"

When we make the decision to follow Christ, we do not know what the future holds. We do not know how Satan is going to tempt us and try hard to put doubts in our minds. Many times, I question God. I ask Him why is He allowing certain things to happen. You are in control; why do You put so much on me? I sometimes feel like I cannot make it through another day. Sometimes, I cannot even pray. I can just say, "Lord have mercy," but when God comes through for me, and I see His handiwork, it strengthens my faith in Him.

So, we made the decision to go to the funeral. We made it above all odds. Yes, there was water everywhere; yes, it was a long journey. Was it worth going to this funeral? Yes! The group of us believed so; therefore, the decision was made, and we proceeded. We saw the need to be of support to our co-worker, and

> *Whatever decision we make in life, there will be consequences to follow—whether good or bad.*

if it meant that we would have to get out of our comfort zones to offer comfort, then that we would do. The decision was made to go forward, and we moved forward in faith.

Whatever decision we make in life, there will be consequences to follow—whether good or bad. We made the decision to go, and even though to us this was a good decision, we will see the consequences that followed. Will these be good consequences or bad? Will our experiences draw us closer to God, or will they pull us away and cause us to question God's existence?

Chapter 5

The Wait

I lived about fifteen minutes from the main road and approximately twenty minutes from Salem and Runaway Bay, where Merlyn and Hirfa lived. I left my house at approximately 8:45 a.m., so by approximately 9:00 a.m., I was waiting for them at my bus stop. They came shortly after 9:00 and very soon, we picked up Veneice in Ocho Rios and were off to the funeral. The areas we lived were tourist areas; therefore, many hotels and resorts lie along the north coast from Runaway Bay, through Salem, and all the way to Ocho Rios. Ocho Rios is one of the major tourist towns in that area. There is also a port there, and cruise ships would dock there every week.

Even though we met with a little rain here and there, most of the journey was okay. The journey was long, but this was understood as we had to drive at a slower speed due to the fact that we were still having rains on and off, and the roads were extremely wet. We played Bible games, and at one point, we were rehearsing the song that we were going to sing at the funeral— "Going Home."

I did not have a reliable car to go on such a long journey, so I had to wait on Merlyn. Was she true to her word? Would she pick me up at the time specified? I could not do anything if she went ahead and left me, so I went and waited on her, hoping that she would keep her word and pick me up at the time agreed upon.

Sometimes the Holy Spirit keeps knocking at our hearts' doors, and we continue to reject Him. We say, "Lord, I cannot serve You now, I am too young. Lord, I have to get married first; Lord, I have to enjoy life first; Christianity is for someone older." We find so many things to say why we cannot serve God today. The scriptures say, "Today if you hear my voice, harden not your heart" (see Heb. 3:15).

I had a very good friend and co-worker, Jackie. She had her life all planned out. One day we were talking, and she said that she was going to serve the Lord. She said she was going to be baptized. I was so happy for her, and as I questioned her, I was saddened. She said she would do all this when she was married. The problem was that there were no plans to get married soon. I tried to encourage her to do it more quickly. She said, yes, when I get married. She said, I am going to become an Adventist.

Jackie resigned from her job and went to work elsewhere. I was in my office one day when a staff member asked me if I knew Jackie. I became alarmed and asked what he meant by, "if I knew Jackie." He told me that she met with an accident and died. I was torn up. I said, Lord, but she is not married yet. What if … I cannot determine her fate. I can only hope that she found time to repent of her sins. She wanted to be baptized, but she was waiting to be married first. Wait can be dangerous. It can be deadly. If we are doing any waiting, we should wait on the Lord, not waiting to get things done before we accept Christ.

We should never wait on another to accept Christ. I was at the bus stop waiting for the ride. If this ride did not come, I would have to go back home because I did not have a reliable car to proceed, and I would miss attending the funeral. When we decide to wait on someone before we accept Christ, what if that person does not show up? What if he takes his own time? Are we still going to wait? Sometimes we do to our own detriment. Let us not wait until we get married, or find the right job, or finish school, or get older before we decide to accept Christ as our Savior. Time waits on no one! Brothers and sisters, let us let go of whatever is holding us down and let God.

The Holy Spirit will not always be with us, and if He keeps knocking at our heart's door, one day, He will leave us, and then we will be doomed because we would have missed out on the opportunity to be saved. James 4:7–8 says, "Submit yourselves therefore to God. Resist the devil, and he will flee from you. Draw nigh to God, and he will draw nigh to you. Cleanse your hands, ye sinners; and purify your hearts, ye double minded."

Chapter 6

Off We Go

By approximately 12:00 noon, we reached Mavis Bank. Driving through this community was breathtaking at times. Mother Nature presented itself to us in many forms—the mountain scenery, the rocks, oh, they were so beautiful! At times, because of the beauty all around, we forgot how bad the roads were. We reached a section of the road where a big rock was hanging from the bank and was almost in the middle of the road. We almost had to squeeze our way through.

I also realized that this was a very small community. The roads were very narrow, and the lashing rain from the previous Thursday was evident on the bushes and the hillsides. There were also areas where it seemed that if the rain should continue to fall, then the banks would start to break away, as the earth was greatly saturated with water from the continuous downpour.

We were now in Mavis Bank, but we were not sure where to go. We did not have a GPS or MapQuest as these devices were not used in Jamaica at the time. We, therefore, called Pastor Willis to inform him that we were now in Mavis Bank. He instructed us to go by the river, and we should not attempt to cross. We had no idea what he meant by us not attempting to cross the river. "Which river?" I questioned myself. We know vehicles do not cross rivers, and we had no other means of transportation to get to the funeral. They did not tell us that they lived across from a river. How were we to cross this river? We were already dressed for the funeral and had no change of clothes suitable to cross any river. We were on the road to a funeral; we had no rivers in mind!

We did not know that Pastor Willis had also communicated this information to Hirfa prior to our starting the journey, and if we had known, maybe we would not have ventured out. We were told to park at the river and wait there for a shuttle to the funeral. When we got to the river, we clearly understood why we could not cross. All the vehicles that were there parked and waited. Afterward, the hearse with the body came, parked, and waited. I did not know what we were waiting for, but we waited. Time seemed to be dragging on, but we patiently, sometimes curiously, waited in the drizzling rain. Other people did not look as curious as we did. It seemed as if they were accustomed to this situation. They did not ask any questions about why they had to wait at the river. They just came by vehicle or on foot and waited. Because we wanted to fit in, we just stopped being so curious and waited patiently like the rest.

Up until this time, we could have chosen to return home, as it was fairly safe to go back from where we were. However, no one made that suggestion, and we just waited there to see what exactly would happen next. Going home was the furthest thing from our minds. Curiosity got the better of us, and we just decided silently that we would wait. I had no intention of leaving, but if I did, I would have had to seek consent from Merlyn, as she was the only one in the group who drove to the funeral.

We learned later that other staff members from NJC came as far as the river but decided to turn back. Some had smaller children with them and others, well, maybe just missed the shuttle!

Our shuttle had finally arrived! A truck came by, and very soon, the casket was placed in it. We then realized that we would be traveling on this truck with the casket to the funeral, as once the casket was placed in it, people started boarding. We went into the truck by climbing sideways on its rails until we were inside. Close to thirty people boarded the truck. Some were left behind as it could not hold everybody. All this time, I thought the church was very nearby. I was told afterward that this was not so. We had to travel for maybe close to an hour to get to the church at Halls Delight.

Halls Delight. I had never heard of any place with such a name. It, however, sounded like a very nice place, so even though we went through all that trouble, I was indeed looking forward to seeing the Halls Delight community.

Chapter 7

Journey to Halls Delight

The truck came, and I realized that this truck was going to cross the river. I found it very funny to see how we were going to be transported to the funeral. I started smiling. I figured that we were going to take another route to the funeral, so even though I felt awkward in the truck, I was happy we were leaving the river. To my surprise, there was no other route to take. I thought that this driver was joking when he was positioning the truck to go across the river. Some men went before the truck at the edge of the river and used sticks to ensure that the wheels of the truck were positioned in the right path. The smile came off my face very quickly when I realized that we were indeed going across in the truck.

The river that we should cross was also the road to the Halls Delight community. The river had overflowed its banks, and only drivers who were familiar with the road surface (driving big units such as a truck) could cross it. There was no road in sight, just a big mass of water that was over six feet deep in some areas.

The men ensured that the truck was positioned in the proper driving space so that the truck would not wash over the river. I was slowly realizing the danger we were in. The truck (a big Leyland—open back/dump) started and moved toward this big mass of swift-moving water. We, at times, felt as if the truck would have washed away. We were told that the driver could only drive in one certain position, and if he missed, then it would have washed away. The water had the truck rocking as if it was a ship set on sail in raging water. I was scared! I held on tightly to one of the rails on the truck.

I started wondering why we made such an irresponsible decision to go in this truck. I asked the Lord to guide us through this short but dangerous journey. I started to think about my family back home. I had two children, and the smaller one, Kara, was only three years old. I left in such a hurry in the morning to meet Merlyn that I did not even give a proper goodbye. Is this the end of my life? Was this how I was going to meet death? *Lord, I am still so young, please have mercy on me*, I silently prayed. *Save me! save me! dear Jesus.* My faith at that time was so weak. I had no hope that this truck would make it to the other side of the road. Finally, we started feeling the tires on earth, and we realized that we were on the other side of the river. Even though it was a very scary cross, we managed to get to the other side, and what took a couple of minutes to cross felt like hours.

The driver, a pastor, drove irresponsibly on a narrow, winding, rough road to Halls Delight. People kept on crying out in fear of their lives. This driving was even more scary than it was crossing the river. We were flung around the corners; people were afraid of the precipices (and there were many), and at times, we felt as if we were going over.

The truck was partly covered at the front section with a tarpaulin, but other people had umbrellas open to try and keep off the rain. Some like me found it uncomfortable as the drops between each umbrella felt big and cold and were unbearable. I had no umbrella, but what was the use? Very soon, those who had umbrellas had no use for them as the wind damaged them soon after the truck started for Halls Delight.

I could no longer hold unto the rails of the truck as every time it went around a corner, people would involuntarily move out of their position, and some were tumbling on others. I managed to get a seat on the casket, so I could not see where I was going as people were all around and could only interpret the responses of the people when they screamed—we were in danger, and silence means out of danger. I vividly remembered a man telling people sitting on the casket to *"come aff Ms. Willis' head nuh. Uno can sit anywhere else but not an har head."* He acted as if the deceased was aware of what was taking place, and she was feeling the weight of the people sitting on her. I scoffed at such an idea because I know the dead know nothing. It was, however, not an appropriate time

Chapter 7: Journey to Halls Delight

to enlighten him concerning his statements.

We reached a section of the road where some people were trying to take out a vehicle that went over the road the night before. We walked a short part of the journey as it was very dangerous for the truck to pass that area fully loaded. The earth was breaking away, and the fully loaded truck would certainly have gone over. Very soon, we were back in the truck. Even though we had passed the worst part of the roads, the journey to the church was still not a pleasant one. It rained all the way to the church, and by the time we reached the church, we were soaked. We had to keep on the cold, wet clothes as there was nothing for us to change into.

> *We walked a short part of the journey as it was very dangerous for the truck to pass that area fully loaded.*

Chapter 8

At the Funeral

Once sitting in the church, apart from feeling cold and wet, one would not believe the hassle we went through to get there. There was just a slight drizzle at this time. People empathized with us when they heard what we went through. Everything seemed quite calm, and soon after, the funeral service began. The music was very loud and distasteful—or was it because I was very wet, cold, and uncomfortable? All this time, the casket was at the back of the church.

The singing ceased shortly afterward, and then the choir, followed by the platform party, marched up followed by the casket. This was somewhat different from all the other funerals that I had attended.

We were called upon as representatives from NJC of Seventh-day Adventists. I brought greetings on behalf of the president and workers of the North Jamaica Conference, and the group of us sang beautifully. The ending of the song— "Going Home" — was even more beautiful than the rest of it, as we totally ruined it. Representatives from other Adventist churches were there—Warsop, Dover, Spring Gardens, and they also did their part. (These people were all from the parish of Trelawny (where Pastor Willis was the pastor). After all the Adventist groups did their part, Pastor Willis did his tribute to his mother. He ended with a beautiful song— "Farther Along."

People spoke highly of the deceased. They said that the only thing that she was afraid of was water, and she got that in abundance at her funeral. As stated in Ecclesiastes 9:10, "For there is no work, nor device, nor knowledge, nor wisdom, in the grave, whither thou goest." The dead know nothing! If Mrs. Willis were aware of what was happening around her, she would have reacted to the situation. In other words, she would get up and run!

During the service, we got the news that the river was rising and that it would be best to leave the area before we could not get out at all. The driver of a minivan decided to take us. We were almost certain that this vehicle was too small to get us across the river, but we were desperate like a drowning man grasping after a straw. We would use any means necessary to get home. We got into the minivan and started out. On reaching the section of the road where the car went over the night before, we realized that the road was now impassable. There were giant cracks in the road as a result of the soil movement, and some of the cracks were almost six feet deep. We had no choice but to return to the funeral service.

We were comforted with the thought that the men in the community would repair the road, and the driver of the truck was going back after the funeral, and we could cross the river in the truck. However, remembering the ride from the river to the church earlier, the thought of going back with it was somewhat disturbing.

Chapter 9

At the Graveside

When the service ended, we boarded the minivan to head toward the graveside, which was about a mile away. We soon had to disembark from the minivan and walked the rest of the way, as the road was impassable. At one time, I was so cold that Pastor Willis lent me his wet jacket—hoping to get some warmth from it but to no avail. I felt cold from inside out.

The deceased was to be interred at the family's plot near the family home, walking distance from the family's house. The house was on a hillside with not many houses beside it. There were thick, luscious bushes and trees surrounding the house and the graveside.

Those at the graveside acted as if there was no rain. Everything went on as planned, and there seemed to be no urgency in getting the work done. Although it was raining, everyone stayed in the rain, singing and clapping (as if there was brilliant sunshine) until the grave was totally sealed. In Jamaica, it is customary for people to leave the church service and go straight to the graveside. Once the pastor commits the body, the congregation would start to sing songs while the men mix the mortar (cement) to make a vault. The singing would cease only when the grave is properly sealed and completed.

We were told that the driver of the truck could not leave early as he was in charge of the sealing of the grave, so we stayed there until everything was completed. This exercise was finished at approximately 6:00 p.m. Feeling happy that the graveside was finished and that we would now be leaving, we were also told that the driver was going up to the house to have some food. We also went to the house. They had food, but nothing that we could eat as none of us ate chicken or curried goat, neither did we drink Manish water (goat's intestines, head, and feet made in soup). This soup is one of the popular dishes that was served at various functions in Jamaica, e.g., funerals, weddings, and dances. Veneice could have eaten the chicken, but she did not want to. We waited for approximately two hours when we were told that the driver was ready.

Chapter 10

On and Off

It could possibly be approximately 8:00 p.m., and it was now dark, and we could not see where we were going. There were no street lights or any other light near the truck. There was a slight drizzle, and we were wet from the journey from the river to the church until that time. Anyway, we went into the truck. The tarpaulin now completely covered the truck, and nothing could be seen clearly, not even the person next to you. I felt scared!! The darkness was so thick that I could almost feel it. There were quite a few people in the truck, but I could not tell where they were. I could only depend on the sense of feeling to determine how close the next person was to me.

People came on, then off, then on again. Merlyn and Veneice came on and off and on and off. I could not see them but recognized their voices. We had to continue calling out for each other because we did not want some of us to be on the truck while the others were off. I came on, off, and on again, after which we heard that there was a fire under the truck. We decided at that point that we would not go down with the truck but that we would stay overnight at the house. It was just too much, and we could not take any more at that point. Many others, including the other Adventists from the churches in Trelawny, decided to stay over as well.

Many times, as Christians, we keep going in and out of the church. We do not see the need to remain in the ark of safety. As soon as someone does us bad, we jump ship. We do not stay in the ship where our protection is sure. James 1:8 says that "A double minded man is unstable in all his ways." We were double-minded because we kept going on and off the truck. We said that we trusted God, but we doubted the means that He gave us to cross the river.

Chapter 10: On and Off

Just as how the truck was rocking in the raging water, our Christian life sometimes is rocky. We are tested by the devil from every front. Sometimes, just as how I could not see where I was going, we cannot see where we are going as Christians. Let us leave our lives in the hands of the Master Driver. He will not lead us into destruction. When we cannot see the path because of the thick cloud of darkness, we still can trust our God. Our Master Driver will drive us through the rocky, stormy, uncertain path into the path of safety.

Our God is in control, so we do not have to see where we are going, and we do not have to "jump truck." We do not have to wait or depend on others to get a response. When we are close to Him, when we approach His throne, He responds directly to us. When we are close to Him, we will have a testimony to share, and we will not have to use somebody else's.

We must stay on the truck even though the drive is rocky and rough. We must stay on the truck when we are criticized and ridiculed. We must stay on the truck as the tempest is raging and the path to travel is uncertain.

> *Our God is in control, so we do not have to see where we are going, and we do not have to "jump truck."*

So many people have jumped truck and were not given the opportunity to return as time ran out on them. Some died in their sins. Some have jumped truck so many times and have been re-baptized so many times that Christianity becomes nothing to them. They do whatever they want to do. Some have one foot in the church and the other outside.

People keep jumping truck because of convenience. They find it easier to stay out so that they can do the things they want to do. Others leave because they cannot find any love in the church. Church people can be very cold and hypocritical, and those who leave cannot endure their scrutiny and judgments. They forget the scripture that says that the wheat and tares will grow together until the day of harvest. Others leave the church because of disobedience. They want to be involved in church activities but want to be a part of the world and what it has to offer. Some leave the church because of gossiping, backbiting, and envy. Others leave because they believe that the church has too many strict rules to follow. Some leave the church because they feel inferior to other members. Some leave the church because they are downright lazy and find it a burden to go in the house of the Lord on His holy Sabbath. Isaiah 58:13--14 says, "If thou turn away thy foot from the sabbath, from doing thy pleasure on my holy day; and call the sabbath a delight, the holy of the Lord, honourable; and shalt honour him, not doing thine own ways, nor finding thine own pleasure, nor speaking thine own words: Then shalt thou delight thyself in the Lord; and I will cause thee to ride upon the high places of the earth, and feed thee with the heritage of Jacob thy father: for the mouth of the Lord hath spoken it."

We need to stop jumping truck. We need to stop going on and off because we do not want to get caught in the middle. We need to stop playing church.

The group of us continued to go on and off, and we made the decision to get off when we realized there was trouble ahead. However, if we had stayed, as uncertain and troublesome as it seemed, we would have crossed the river that very night. Other people stayed on, and they went across the river and were not subjected to the challenges that were waiting for us.

Let us not wait until our problems overcome us before we try to run back to the ark of safety. We might just not be able to return. Let us stay in the ark where our souls can be nurtured and nourished so that when we are tempted, when the sea billows roll, we would be steadfast, unmoveable, and we would not be blown away by contrary winds of doctrine. Yes, in the truck, we may be flung to and fro, and at times, we may not even have a church member whom we can depend on to help us. Sometimes the responses of members are the very ones that may lead us astray. Let us not wait on the responses of others to determine the kind of relationship that we want to have with Jesus. We may be sitting in the middle of the congregation enveloped by the gossiping, backbiting, coldness, and cruelty of others, and we may seem that we cannot find a strong footing. Do not give up! God is carrying you. As rocky as it may seem, you will make it if you hold onto God.

1 John 1:9 says, "If we confess our sins, he is faithful and just to forgive us our sins, and to cleanse us from all unrighteousness." I encourage my young friends and my older friends to stay on the truck because this truck is destined only for the heavenly kingdom. Let us keep our eyes on Jesus because when we do this, we will not even realize when the truck is rocking. Let us stop going on and off. Let us remain in the ark of safety because in it, there is peace.

Chapter 11

Overnighting

We went back to the house and informed Pastor Willis of our decision to stay overnight. It was difficult to find dry clothes as only a young lady and her boyfriend (a son of the deceased) lived at the house, and her kind of clothes would not be suitable for us. Her clothing was more the party type—skimpy and close-fitting. Pastor Willis and his family were staying there for a few days, and after some amount of search, Pastor Willis' wife found some of her and her husband's clothes for each of us, and we soon changed into these dry clothes. The other people had to stay in their wet clothes right through the night. We had rice and peas and peppermint tea for dinner, and soon, we were off to bed.

The house was very small, and even though there were approximately three bedrooms, one bathroom, and a living room, the rooms were very small. All the bedrooms put together would make one big master bedroom.

The sleeping arrangement was very difficult. All four of us, including the young lady of the house and her six-week-old baby, had to sleep on one double-sized bed. Most of the others maintained a sitting position throughout the night. In light of the child's age, the baby and her mother got more than half of the bed. The other less-than-half was for the four of us. We were so closely knitted together on the bed that no one person could turn. It was good that all four of us were of a small to medium built. We all laid in the same direction, and I would give out the sound "Turning Time," and then everybody would turn at the same time. This was done repeatedly throughout the night. Sometimes the side that I laid on ached, but we could only turn at "Turning Time." Once, I tried going on my back before "Turning Time," but to no avail.

Chapter 11: Overnighting

I had to go back in the same position and waited with the aching side until it was time to turn.

About midnight, we heard a sound, and Veneice dashed out of bed. I followed behind her. Someone said that it sounded like a mudslide. We asked the young lady what it was, and she told us it was water on the tarpaulin outside at the back of the house that was making that sound. She then covered up and went back to sleep. We were still troubled as it sounded very much like mud. But I thought that the young lady should be more aware of what it was, and as she was not perturbed about the situation, we hesitantly went back to bed. We went back to sleep. I then heard talking. I heard an old lady asking:

> *"What time is it?"* Somebody replied, *"3 o'clock."* The lady then said,
> *"Fram di time till now wi sleeping is honly tree a clack, anyway, mek wi try again."*

Very soon, all were sleeping, and there was total silence, only the rain sometimes making lashing sounds, sometimes light sounds, sometimes pouring sounds, but all through the night, it rained. I thanked God that there were no thunderstorms because I am very scared of lightning and thunder.

This situation brought the four of us closer together as friends and co-workers. We felt as family, and I believe that this special bond will not be broken but will last forever. I pray it lasts.

Chapter 12

Morning at Halls Delight

After a very eventful night, we were up at dawn. We had devotions, but the singing was not very encouraging. Uncertainty and anxiety could be felt in the room, and it interfered with the worship service. It was only natural for us to be worried at that point because of what we went through and to be anxious about what awaited us. I remembered Merlyn encouraging us that we needed to give God thanks in spite of the situation, as He had brought us safely through the terrible ordeal from the night before.

In our lives it does not matter the miracles the Lord has done; as soon as we meet upon another trial or tribulation, we forget what God did for us previously. It was just the day before that God moved mightily for us, and it seemed we had already forgotten. We were like the children of Israel during the passage from Egypt to the promised land. The Lord worked miracles after miracles, and with every trial, they complained. What else must our heavenly Father do for us to have our total trust and dependence in Him? We forgot how He protected us in the truck when we were crossing the river, how He gave us provision to stay overnight, and how He provided dry clothes. Yes, we easily forgot and became anxious about the unknown. Philippians 4:6–7 reminds us that we should "Be careful for nothing; but in everything by prayer and supplication with thanksgiving let our requests be made known unto God. And the peace of God, which passeth all understanding, shall keep our hearts and minds through Christ Jesus."

We sang some more songs; then, each person gave a Bible verse. After which, Pastor Willis gave an exhortation. We then sang the prayer chorus, "Trust in the Lord with all of your heart and lean not to your own understanding, but in all thy ways acknowledge

Chapter 12: Morning at Halls Delight

Him and He shall direct thy path." We all sensed the feeling, and all had an implied agreement that we needed divine direction and protection to take us out of Halls Delight. We all sensed that trouble was not yet over, so we approached God's throne. I offered the first prayer, and Pastor Willis then gave the closing one. The president of NJC got news of the problem we were in, and he called us to reassure us that he was praying. He encouraged us that we should not worry but should allow the Lord to lead and direct us.

We went straight back to bed, and after a while, we got up. We did not have toothbrushes, so we just had a mint sweet for our toothpaste. We had no bath but were certain that the rain would be our shower for that morning and that we would get it in abundance. That took care of that. We were then served bread, steamed cabbage, and mint tea for our breakfast, which we enjoyed very much. In a short while, Hirfa brought some garbage bags for us to put our wet clothes in. We, however, kept them as we knew that we would find better use for them. We later used them as coats and hats, as when we were ready to leave, the rain was still falling.

God gave us the opportunity more than once to avoid or get away from this terrible ordeal. First of all, we were warned that Saturday night about the blockage in Mavis Bank, but we did not take heed. Secondly, when confronted with having to cross the river, any well-thinking person would have turned back at this point. We, however, chose not to. What were we thinking of? What were we trying to prove? Would our God still make a way for us even though we made these foolish decisions? Sometimes, as Christians, we allow certain trials and tribulations to come upon us, then we call on the Lord for help. We purposely sin against our God. We tell lies, we covet, we backbite, we bear false witness against our neighbors, we hate. We do all these things, but once we sincerely ask God to forgive us, He is there waiting with open arms to take us back into His fold. Yes, like us on this journey, we had a choice not to go to Halls Delight, but we did anyway.

Every time we are tempted, the Holy Spirit is there to point us to Christ and to make the right decision. "There hath no temptation taken you but such as is common to man: but God is faithful, who will not suffer you to be tempted above that ye are able; but will

> *Every time we are tempted, the Holy Spirit is there to point us to Christ and to make the right decision.*

with the temptation also make a way to escape, that ye may be able to bear it" (1 Cor. 10:13). The Lord has always presented a way out of our temptations, but, sad to say, many times, we yield to Satan and fall into the snares and traps he has set for us. Let us not yield to temptations, for yielding is sin. Let us not even entertain these temptations. Sometimes we would not have sinned, but because we continue to think about the situation, we linger, and the end result is sin. Let us ask the Lord to immediately dismiss any thought that would lead us to sin. We should remember that our thoughts eventually lead to action. Sometimes when we sin, we feel so hopeless and do not believe our heavenly Father will forgive us. We made such poor decisions taking this journey. Would our God come to our rescue from Halls Delight?

Chapter 13

Departure from Halls Delight

The entire rural community of Halls Delight was cut off from the surrounding communities and major towns. We were trapped inside, and we did not know how to get out. The rain continued pouring, and things looked hopeless. We then found out that the young lady of the house was not from Halls Delight but came there to live from a nearby town. She said despite the remoteness of the area and the poor conditions when it rains, which occurs quite often, she liked the area. She said that when the weather gets as bad as it was during the time we were there, people with health emergencies would be airlifted and taken to the hospitals. Students would just have to wait until the passage was safe for them to return to school.

When it was safe enough, some skilled men would offer their services by taking those who had to go out on their backs across the river. Even if we wanted them to do the same for us, they would not have done so, as they said that it was too dangerous at the time to do it. *Wow!* I said to myself. This condition disgusted me, but the people living in the community accepted it and were contented living there. They seemed quite happy.

I am not saying that we were rich, but the areas we live in were 100 percent better than this community, yet we find so many things to complain about. These people knew their limitations; they did not fuss nor worry; they just accepted things the way they were and lived simply and happily. Some of them (like the young lady) may have the opportunity to leave but, for whatever reason, choose to stay and are contented with their living conditions. If only I could live by that example. As Christians, we should not glory in extravagance or pomp and pride, but we must live in humility and endeavor to live a simple and happy life, even amidst our trials. Every aspect of our lives should reflect the loving God that we serve.

Even though we were having such difficulty getting home, the group of four had no regrets about going to the funeral because Pastor Willis was a dear pastor to us, and we wanted to give him our support and to show him how much we love and appreciate him and his family.

We were told that the only way to get out of the community was to bypass the river by going up in the mountains. *Mountains?* I said to myself. *My God, what is happening?* First, it was rivers, now mountains!! My mind then flashed back on my family at home, and I was now ready to climb any mountain to get home. Hope came alive! I was now ready for the mountain challenge because I knew that God would keep all of us safe and take us through.

We stepped out in the rain, and seeing that no vehicle could come for us because of the deteriorated road surface, we decided to walk all the way to the river. So, at 8:45 a.m., we started off.

Chapter 13: Departure from Halls Delight

Pastor Willis and his wife were with us. Pastor Willis was accompanying us for a part of the journey, but his wife had to go back home to Trelawny as she had to report to work the following day. We also had to report to work the following day. At this point, the rain was still falling, and we were so accustomed to being battered by the rain that it became a normal experience for us. We were no longer bothered by the water beating onto our bodies. Very soon, we all got soaked again. There came my bath! During our walk, some people who wanted to relieve themselves just stopped walking and stooped down—in their clothes! Better yet, others just did it as they continued walking.

We went through a shortcut, and at the end of it, I saw a lady who told us that we had a little less than three miles more to reach the river. I asked her if she could give us some dry clothes, but she said she did not live nearby but was going to the store to get some groceries.

We were very far ahead of the rest of the group, so we slowed down and waited for them to catch up with us. After walking what seemed like a short distance, to my surprise, I was hearing a familiar sound. The sound of the river! We were very near! I liked hearing the river this time as it reminded me that I was indeed going home. I felt joyful. We saw some ladies at a nearby grocery store who warned us that we should not attempt to cross the river. They said that it was still very dangerous as the flow was too swift for us to try and go across. They warned that we might lose our lives if we insisted. We told them that we were not crossing the river, but we learned that it could be bypassed by going through the mountains. They advised us not to do so either, as it was very dangerous, and the earth was soft and was breaking away into the river. Some people were saying that it was okay, while others warned us not to bypass the river. What should we do? I was not about to let these people quench the joy that was bubbling up in me—the joy of knowing that I was truly on my way home.

I should say that the earth was not what we are accustomed to. It was more sand-like (similar to the earth where I presently live in Sumter, South Carolina), and the stones seemed as if they could be easily crushed with the hand. The ladies said we should turn back to Halls Delight. Another lady offered to give us shelter in a nearby church. I took one look at the church building and felt depressed. I was certain that the building was leaking, and I thought to myself, *Could the previous night repeat itself?* I was more worried to have a repeat of the previous night than to bypass the river. We all had a strong desire to go home.

I decided that I was not going back to Halls Delight, neither was I going to stay in the church building. There were no more dry clothes at Halls Delight for us at the house, the thought of the sleeping arrangement at Halls Delight, the thought of sleeping in the little old broken-down church, the thought of being treated like refugees gave us the determination to proceed to the river! There was never any fear, worry, or murmuring, or regrets coming from any of us—only the determination to go forward, to go home. We moved away from the group of ladies as we thought that this was doing us no good. We moved away from discouragement. Ellen G. White, in the book, *Selected Messages*, Book 2, p. 314, says that we should "keep company with the soundest Christians. Choose not the pretentious instructors or pupils, but those who show the deepest piety, those who have a spirit of intelligence in the things of God." We did not believe that the ladies were giving us sound message from God but were just giving their opinions. Even though we might have seemed unwise, we felt that God had promised us direction through that day, so we moved away from anything that would cause discouragement or cause us to change our minds about God's promises.

We must be careful who we keep company with. Everybody goes to church for a different reason. Satan has his people in the churches, and we do not want to keep company with those who will implant negative thoughts in our minds. We do not want to be in company with someone who would offer drugs or alcohol or someone who does not see anything wrong with anything. These are discouragements, and just as how we moved away from this discouragement, we should do the very same in our Christian walk.

There are Satan's emissaries in the church, and some do nothing but cause discouragements, fights, and confusions within the body of Christ. Some members are very hypocritical because they

Chapter 13: Departure from Halls Delight

say one thing but do the total opposite. These hypocrites are like the praying mantises. A praying mantis is an insect, a ferocious killer that looks as if it is praying but, in fact, is not. It hides behind plant leaves, waiting to attack any insect or anything in their paths. They will eat anything, including poisonous insects and other mantises. These church members appear to be holy and look sincere in their attire; however, they are quick to take part in evil discussions against others while they are engaged in church activities. From the frontal view, it seems that they are working for the Master; however, they use their poisonous tongues to kill, backbite, and to slander. These members envy and hate and fight against the work of God. These are the ones we should be wary of. We should ask God to give us a spirit of discernment so we can choose carefully and know when the actions of people have motives other than to work for Jesus. We must choose to associate with people who will help to uplift us and encourage us as we continue on our spiritual journey. We must also pray to God and ask Him to help us that to others, we are not seen as the praying mantises but should live in obedience to His will.

As we neared the river, we met a young man who told us that we could indeed bypass the river, and he showed us one of two shortcuts that we could take. He said that a group was ahead of us. After much begging for him to walk with us, he decided to take us a part of the journey as we had no idea where we were going. He said that he could not go all the way, as he was hungry and needed food. He followed us through the shortcut, and just as he was about to leave us, the Lord provided us with two other guides. The two guides also did not want to follow us, but after much deliberation, they promised to take us a part of the journey.

Did these people have legitimate reasons for not wanting to accompany us, or were they scared to risk their lives in showing us the way? As Christians, we should be ready to risk our lives to point someone to Jesus. We should be willing to go in any volatile, drug-infested community to bring people to Christ. We should be willing to take part in evangelistic meetings and use every means possible to witness for the Lord. We should be willing to go to other countries when the need arises to witness for Christ, whether through health ministry, education, or evangelism. We should not be reluctant as the people were who did not want to show us the way. We profess to be Christians, so we should be ever ready to come out of our comfort zones and be like soldiers in the army for the Lord. I am nowhere near this, but I pray that the Lord will give me the strength to purpose in my mind to go where He leads me so that I may witness for Him.

All this time, Hirfa and I thought that Merlyn and Veneice were with the first group. As we started moving forward, we saw Merlyn and Veneice approaching us. They caught us just in time as we ventured to bypass the river. I could not afford to lose Merlyn as she was the only driver. It would be useless crossing the river and leaving her behind, as I would still be left stranded at Mavis Bank.

Chapter 14

The Climb

It should be noted that some members in our group were elderly men and some plus-sized women, and the next stage of our travel would be of concern especially for this group. I overheard the two guides discussing between themselves as to whether or not the elderly men and the bigger-sized women could make the journey. They both agreed that if these people wanted to make it home, then they would have to. I realized then that we were in for a change, but I kept this to myself. Up to this point, we were assisted by the men in crossing a smaller part of the river, and even though it was nothing compared to the big river, it was still difficult to cross. The water was swift and strong on our feet, and I had to hold onto the hand of one of the guides with a firm grip so as not to get washed away into the bigger river that was lying in wait for us.

One of the guides, at a distance, showed me where we were going to climb and said he was going to leave us at that point. I did not take serious note of where we were going to climb until we were immediately in front. I did not take serious note of this until we came face to face with a huge rock. One of the gentlemen said to me, "You are going up there." I looked but did not see a path, so I asked, "Where?" He showed me again, and I realized that we had very tough times ahead. We were staring at an almost ninety-degree inclination that we had to climb.

Before the climb, the guides showed us where to go. We were instructed to climb up the mountain until we reach some banana trees. We would go down through an iron gate, then cross the last part of the river on a bridge that was on the other side. After crossing the bridge, we would then journey on the right side of the river to where the car was parked. It seemed quite easy at the time.

> *The water was swift and strong on our feet, and I had to hold onto the hand of one of the guides with a firm grip so as not to get washed away into the bigger river that was lying in wait for us.*

There was a huge rock in front of us, and to one side of the rock were some barky strings (rope-like—approximately six inches thick). We had to stand and look up at the rock at a ninety-degree angle as if we were almost looking in the sky. We could not touch the rock from the ground as there was no land there, and the river was directly beneath the rock. We were standing on some smaller rocks a little way from the huge one. One of the gentlemen jumped and caught the strings. He held on to the strings with one hand and held out his other hand for me to join him. I hesitated but was motivated by the thought that I was really going home. I did not find it difficult to do so because, as a child, I enjoyed climbing trees and engaged in activities that were considered to be for boys. It was an adventure that, deep down, I wanted to try. I reached for his hand, and he pulled me toward him. I realized I had to hold fast onto the barky strings. I clung to these rope-like strings for dear life and started climbing them as there was nothing else to climb. If I should fall, I would go straight into the gushing river that was hungrily waiting to devour us.

It is amazing how the Lord always provides for us in simple ways. The rock could have been there without the strings beside it, and if this were the case, there would have been nowhere to climb, and we would have had to turn back to Halls Delight—where there was no delight.

Why can't I learn to put total trust in God? There is nothing too huge or insignificant for Him to handle. He looked in time and saw that we would need to use that route to get out of Halls Delight, and He made the provision so long before we needed them. God knew even before we were born that the time would come when we would have a need to climb those barky strings. Better yet, God, even before man sinned, put in the plan of salvation. We serve a proactive Creator and not a reactive one. We serve a God who is orderly. He looked beyond our faults and saw our needs. We were in need even though we may have made a foolish decision to attend the funeral because of the weather conditions. Yet God provided for us. Yet God protected us. Yet God, yet God. We serve a loving and caring God. We serve a God who is in control of nature and this vast universe.

Nothing was created by chance. Everything that our heavenly Father fashioned is here for a purpose. Many times, we slight or disregard the little things until we are in need of them, and then we see their importance. We should give thanks for the fresh air, for the sense of smell, for little members of our bodies such as our fingers, toes, eyelashes because, at times, only when one of these little members get hurt and our entire body aches, do we realize their importance.

We should give God thanks and praise for everything, even in our trials. We should give thanks for those who are trying to bring us down. Give thanks for our enemies, the little food we have because we could not have had any; the little money we have because we could not have had any; the disobedient children because we could have been childless; the little place we have to sleep because we could have been homeless. We should give Him thanks and praise for the aches and pains because we are alive, and this shows that we still have the sense of feeling! We should praise Him even for the coronavirus because it allows us to spend more time with our Father and our families. We thanked Him for the huge rock and the barky strings beside it because that was the means to get us across the raging river. There are so many things to give God thanks for! Instead of worrying, we should praise Him for our troubles and hold Him to the promises that He made to us.

David, in Psalm 37:25, said, "I have been young, and now am old; yet have I not seen the righteous forsaken, nor his seed begging bread." As a Christian, I know my Provider has always been with my family and me, so I am thankful to Him. I am thankful for life's trials, and I pray that He continues to guide and direct my family and that we will keep Him before us at all times. We should give thanks even when we cannot make sense of the situation. We should give Him thanks when the way is dark, and we cannot see. We did not murmur when we saw those strings beside the rock. We thanked God that we were able to use these rope-like strings as stepping stones to get home. This would not have been our first choice of going home, but this was the one the Lord had in store, and we trusted Him and proceeded. Even though we messed up, the Lord was there, ready to take us out safely.

When trials are set in our way, if we have an attitude of praise and trust, we will conquer much easier and quicker than when we allow self to step in. If the children of Israel were not so disobedient, they would not have spent all of forty years wandering in the wilderness. All of forty years when Canaan was only a couple of weeks in reach. We must remember that our trials are not our own, and when we give them to God Almighty, victory is ours!

We were now fully depending on our God as we realized that this problem was too huge for us to solve. We realized that it would only get messier if we tried to work it out on our own, so with faith and trust and a determination to go home, we climbed these barky strings. With each and every climb, we knew we were a climb nearer home.

In our Christian walk, with each and every step we make, we know we are nearer home. We know that the coming of our Lord and Savior Jesus Christ is so near, so we, therefore, must take steps closer and closer to building a Christ-like character as only such character can take us into the kingdom of God. We have to make the climb out of sin into salvation. Satan will let this climb look impossible, but if we allow the Lord, all He expects us to do is to put the first foot forward. He will not force us, but when we make the effort, He will be there to guide us through.

We might be in some relationships that are so entangled that we do not believe that we can be set free. We might choose not to climb because of the job we have, and we are scared that we will not be able to get the Sabbath off. We might be convinced of the Sabbath, but because of the offices we hold in other churches, we do not want to make the climb. Let us make the climb each day to be one step closer to God. Let us climb out of doubt into faith and trust. Let us climb out of discouragement into confidence and

Chapter 14: The Climb

determination. Let us climb out of worry and fear into boldness and bravery. Let us climb! When it looks dark, and we cannot see, climb. When we are discouraged and talked about, and we know that deep down, we are innocent of what we are being accused of, climb. When we feel as if God is not near us, climb. When we feel that Satan is attacking us on every side, climb. Trust God and make the climb, and keep climbing each and every day for the rest of our lives.

All we need to do is to put one foot forward, and our God will make a way for us. He has sent His only begotten Son, Jesus, to die in our stead. Jesus is the way, the truth, and the life. Yes, that's the way to our heavenly Father. All we need to do is to climb. Climb out of sin and shame and condemnation and climb into life eternal with Jesus. The choice is ours, brothers and sisters; let us start to make that climb today.

Chapter 15

From the Rock to the Bridge

I was leading the group at this point, and with every climb, we went steeper and steeper up the mountains. At some areas, there was nothing to hold onto, and I had to dig my fingers in the already-saturated earth to cling on for life as with one slippage, I could find myself in the river.

Merlyn lost her pair of over-sized jeans that she got from Pastor Willis while trying to climb on the strings to get over the huge rock. She had on little shorts under the pants, and that was all she had left. The river swallowed up the pants. Hirfa was even worse as she only had on her panties under a big shirt. However, everyone was successful in climbing up the rock, even the older men and bigger-sized women! All were determined to go home. After a good while of climbing, sometimes on my belly, finally the banana trees appeared. I was so happy that I shouted out, "I see the banana trees, I see the banana trees."

We passed the banana trees, went through the iron gate, and then had to pass some pig pens. We had to walk in the pig mess. It was horrible. Everything in the pen seemed to have washed down in our path. I had on my slippers, so the horrible mess was everywhere on my feet and between my toes. I think I could comfortably say that every one of us were Adventists. Just to think of pig and Adventists. These two words just do not go together. However, I should say that farther in our travel, we passed some more pig-pens but got through with ease as we were now accustomed to the situation.

We crossed the bridge, and in doing that, we also finally crossed the river, but to our dismay, we were still very far from the car. It seemed that the river was still slightly in the middle, and we had to go sideways (a path very near to the right of the river) to get to the car. This could be close to another two miles. We started going in the direction we were told to go, but when we reached a point, we came upon some elderly men of the community, who told us to turn back and go up into the hills as there was serious breaking away of the earth through this passage, and it would surely take us over into the angry river. As we stood there, we watched as the sides of the pathway broke away into the river. That was exactly where we should have walked. The path was already narrow, and with the breakaway, it became impossible for us to proceed. Any added weight on the ground would definitely cause more break away into the river as well. But this was where the two guides instructed us to go! What should we do now?

We could not turn back as it was too dangerous to go back down the hill, and also, we would have to deal with the huge rock. That was definitely not an option at this point. These locals were not willing to accompany us because of the danger that was lurking. We were alone and did not know what to do. We were advised that climbing up the mountain was still very dangerous. Should we turn back, or should we proceed up the hill? We remembered the experience coming up the mountains from the river, and seeing that it was not a pleasant one, we chose the latter. We did not know what lay ahead. We did not even know where to go, but one thing we were certain of was that our heavenly Father was in the lead, and we, therefore, exercised our trust and faith in Him. We were now putting into action the songs we sung that morning and the one done at the funeral— "Trust in the Lord" and "Going Home."

So up in the hills, we went. I was still in the lead. We walked a long distance. At one point there was a deep precipice on the left of the path that I had to shout several times to those behind me, "Keep to the right, keep to the right." We kept pressing on, but not one of us knew where we were going.

I was still leading the way when I stepped into what felt like quicksand. Something inside the mud kept pulling at my foot as if it wanted to pull me in. Praise the Lord, I managed to pull the foot out. Shortly afterward, my foot got stuck in it again. I tried to take the foot out with my slippers on, but I could not do so. I lost one foot of my slippers in this quicksand-like substance. I tried stirring the area with a stick to find that slipper, but I could not find it. I just threw the other foot in the mud and went on walking—barefooted! I had only my heels left, and they were not ideal for this situation. We followed the tracks until sometimes no track was visible. I ended up in prickles—barefooted! I had to call out,

"Don't come this side—macka!"

Finally, we were in this large hot pepper field. There was a small blue house that we had to pass before reaching the peppers. For a few minutes, we felt happy that someone at the house would give us some sense of direction, as, at this point, we felt helpless and totally lost. We called out to the occupants of the house with great anticipation, but soon afterward, we realized that no one was living there. There were no curtains at the windows ... no glass in the windows ... no sign of life. *No one is living here?* I questioned myself. I felt disappointed.

Chapter 15: From the Rock to the Bridge

There was no way out, nothing to do but just to look at hot peppers—red peppers, green peppers, yellow peppers, big peppers, small peppers. I was tempted to take some of these peppers as they were looking quite good, and I love eating hot country peppers, but a still, calm voice reminded me that this act was called stealing, and this would also not help the situation we were presently in. We felt trapped, with no way out. Not knowing what to do, we decided to call upon our great Leader, who has led us thus far. Merlyn approached God's throne on our behalf.

> *We felt trapped, with no way out.*

Chapter 16

The Prayer

Merlyn's prayer was a simple one. She prayed and asked the Lord to send someone to show us the way as we were now helpless and did not know what to do or where to go from here. It was a few of us who prayed as some people were still behind, trying to catch up with us. This included Pastor Willis and his wife.

I felt the presence of God in our midst while we prayed. We believed that the Lord was going to make a way of escape for us as He had been doing ever since we went to Halls Delight. He made a way of escape for Daniel and the three Hebrew boys. He made a way for Paul when he was in prison; He made a way for Noah to

Chapter 16: The Prayer

save him and his family; He made a way for Jonah, even though he was disobedient and did not do as God commanded. He made a way for baby Moses, for Joseph, for Elijah to be fed by ravens, Queen Esther, the children of Israel ... I could go on and on, but one thing is certain, He is the same God as He was then, and we knew He would continue to make a way of escape for us.

Our prayers were about to be answered. Shortly afterward, one of the members of the group, who was behind, caught up with us and moved in the opposite direction. He shouted out, "Come to this side. I see a house." Veneice kept on asking him where the house was and also where he was, but all he kept on saying was that we should come and see the house. We were in the middle of the mountain. All that could be seen, apart from the old blue house, were bushes, big trees, and colorful peppers. There was no other sign of life.

However, while moving in the direction of our counterpart, a gentleman with a cutlass (machete) came from "out of the blue," and we flocked him and bombarded him with questions as to how we could reach the other side of the river at Mavis Bank. All this time, we still did not see the house that the young man saw. He, too, was puzzled as he no longer saw it.

Even though the man with the machete said he had a far distance to go home, he decided to take us a part of the journey as he realized that we would not be able to find it on our own. I believe that the Holy Spirit showed our friend the house so that we could see this man. If we did not turn in that direction, we could have missed him.

This reminded me that we should be very specific when we pray. Merlyn, even though it seemed impossible, asked God for someone to come and show us the way. There was no house in the area, only bushes and trees. There were no visible tracks, and because it was raining continuously for approximately four days now, the possibility of seeing someone in those bushes was dim. With all this against us, Merlyn still asked the Lord to send someone to help us, and we believed that He would answer our prayers. Praise the Lord, God answered our prayer in five minutes!

"To every sincere prayer an answer will come. It may not come just as you desire, or at the time you look for it; but it will come in the way and at the time that will best meet your need. ... God answers, not always to your expectations, but always for your good" (*Messages to Young People*, p. 250). James 5:16 says, "The effectual fervent prayer of a righteous man availeth much."

We should not only be specific when praying to God but also we must have faith and believe that it will be according to His will. We were not only reminded that day that prayer moves mountains but prayer also moves us out of the mountains. Whatever the difficulty in life is, prayer and faith can change it. This is evident in Mark 11:22–23, which says, "So Jesus answered and said to them, 'Have faith in God. For assuredly, I say to you, whoever says to this mountain, "Be removed and be cast into the sea," and does not doubt in his heart, but believes that those things he says will be done, he will have whatever he says'" (NKJV).

Whenever our problems are so huge and it seems that there is no way out, we should pray. In Daniel chapter 6, Daniel purposed in his heart to pray even when there was danger lurking. The decree was made that prayer should be made only to the king. This decree went against Daniel's faith, and if he were caught praying to his God, he would be thrown into the lions' den. Yet Daniel exercised all faith in God. He did not hide and pray, but he continued as he normally would—by opening up his windows. He prayed, and even though he was caught and had to face the consequences, God delivered him.

When perplexities arise, and difficulties confront you, look not for help to humanity. Trust all with God. The practice of telling our difficulties to others only makes us weak, and brings no strength to them. It lays upon them the burden of our spiritual infirmities, which they cannot relieve. We seek the strength of erring, finite man, when we might have the strength of the unerring, infinite God. (*Christ's Object Lessons*, p. 146)

When It Seems ...

When it seems so dark that you cannot see,
When to you the cross you carry, you can't bear,

Chapter 16: The Prayer

When to you the load you carry is as wide as the sea,
And at times, these problems might cause a tear.

When you seem to be on a road that has no return,
And doubts and fears envelope your path,
When loved ones you miss cause you to feel down,
God is there all the time, more so at the aftermath.

When it seems you cannot make it, pray!
With God, you can do it! Stay on your knee!
My God will help you find your way,
I know! He has done it so often for me.

With God, you can climb all the mountains in your life,
With God, you can cross the deep, wide, raging sea,
With God, it does not matter what heartache and strife,
Stay with Him, stay with Him; this is my plea!
By: Carline Samuels

There were times my family had some heavy crosses to carry. Sometimes we prayed for a long time, and it seemed that God was not even hearing us. Sometimes we felt like questioning Him, and the devil tempted us to give up on Him. But we continued to hold on. We did not give in to feelings, but we used past experience and the Word of God to help us hold onto what we could not see. We stayed with God on our knees and in our hearts, and He came right on time, every time.

My youngest sister, Nathalie Francis (Natty), who resided in Georgia, battled lupus for thirteen years. This caused her health to deteriorate to the point where she spent a lot of time in the hospital. At one stay, she was placed on a life support machine for more than three months. She had heart failures, and it seemed everything was going in the wrong direction. We, however, did not give up hope on Natty. We prayed, and even when it seemed there was no hope, we prayed. When the doctor told my husband that it was a 50/50 percent chance of recovery, I gave God thanks for that 50 percent chance she had to live. I did not look at the other

50 percent. We prayed and praised. Through answered prayer, we saw God's handiwork. My sister recovered from that illness at that time. She lived another ten years before she succumbed to her illness in 2018. My prayer was that she would have surrendered her all to the Lord and made her calling and election sure. Hannah prayed to the Lord for a male child. She was specific in her request. She also made a promise to God that if He blessed her womb, then she would give back to Him her blessing. The Lord blessed Hannah, and she kept her promise to Him. Prayer moves mountains, and it also moves us out of the mountains.

It must have been hard for Jochebed, the mother of Moses, when she realized that all the baby boys were being killed. She prayed to the Lord, and she also made that climb. She prayed that the Lord would save her baby, and He did. How could her baby be saved when it was the decree that all the baby boys should be killed? Where could she hide this baby? We all know that babies do not keep silent. They cry when they are happy, hungry, or sad. How would she keep the baby quiet? Yet the Lord in His infinite wisdom used the very people who were killing these babies to spare Moses' life.

> Prayer is the answer to every problem in life. It puts us in tune with divine wisdom, which knows how to adjust everything perfectly. So often we do not pray in certain situations, because from our standpoint the outlook is hopeless. But nothing is impossible with God. Nothing too entangled that it cannot be remedied. No human relationship is too strained for God to bring about reconciliation and understanding: no habit too deep rooted that it cannot be overcome. No one is so weak that he cannot be strong: No one is so ill that he cannot be healed. No mind is so dull that it cannot be made brilliant. Whatever we need, if we trust God, He will supply it. If anything is causing worry, and anxiety, let us stop rehearsing the difficulty and trust God for healing, love and power. (*The Daily Word,* June 18, 1952)

Sometimes the way we want God to answer our prayers is not the way He answers them. We may become anxious, and the devil will press on us that our heavenly Father is not hearing us. We must believe that even when the prayers are not answered the way we want Him to answer them, they are still being answered. He knows what's best for us and answers according to His will. We should have trust in God that even when the prayers are not answered as to how we want it, we know that He has our best interest in heart. My dad, Vincent Francis, passed away in August 2020 from the coronavirus. He was eighty-nine years of age and had no underlying illnesses. We prayed that he would recover. Sometimes when I showed weakness and doubt, my son Kevaun would encourage me to have faith and continue to pray. However, God allowed my father to fall asleep. I still trust Him because I prayed for healing, and God saw that putting him to sleep was the best healing. I praise Jehovah for answering my prayer!

Our God can make any path clear. He can make the crooked straight and the rough smooth. It does not matter how deep-rooted we are in our problems, if we ask the Lord to intervene, He will. Let us go boldly before our heavenly Father and let Him know what we are in need of. He is interested in the very smallest details of our lives. He loves us so much and wants to help us. In 1 John 5:14–15, it says, "And this is the confidence that we have in him, that, if we ask any thing according to his will, he heareth us: And if we know that he hear us, whatsoever we ask, we know that we have the petitions that we desired of him."

Let us, therefore, have the confidence in God. When our relationships go bad, let us have confidence in Him. When we are abused by our spouses, let us have confidence in Him; when we cannot find work because we choose to keep the Sabbath holy, have confidence. If we are pressured by our peers or being bullied on social media, have confidence in God. He can remedy the situation. Those who are stricken with sicknesses like cancer, HIV/AIDS, lupus, hypertension, diabetes, heart disease, those who have lost loved ones, let us have that confidence that our heavenly Father has heard us and that He will answer on time, according to His will. Remember Hebrews 10:35 (KJV) says, "Cast not away therefore your confidence, which hath great recompence of reward."

When we do this, we will have less time to worry and more time to take our burdens to the Lord. Brothers and sisters, let us be specific in what we want to ask the Lord for. He already knows what we need, but when we exercise this faith and bring our requests, our faith will be strengthened when the Lord answers our prayers.

> **Brothers and sisters, let us be specific in what we want to ask the Lord for.**

Let us pray that the Lord will prick our hearts, and we will follow His directions. Let us pray that we will develop Christ-like characters as only this will take us to heaven. Let us pray that our children will have the desire to study the Word of God and that with the help of the Holy Spirit, they will choose to live lives that are pleasing to God in this world of sin and sorrow. Let us pray that our children will not develop the taste for worldly gains and pleasure, for these will come at a cost and will burn in the lake of fire. Let us pray for our family members and friends who are sick and are halting between two opinions. Pray for those who have not yet accepted Christ that they will do so before it is too late. Let us pray for health and strength and that we will continue to remain true to Him even when trials and tribulations come our way. Let us pray without ceasing. Let us pray every day.

Finally, we left the pepper field and were behind this man, who was leading us out of that area. At one point I touched him to see if he was an angel. He felt real to me. We would have never found the way out as the grass on both sides covered the track, and we had to actually bend to go through the track as if we were going through a tunnel. The grass was wet and cold from the constant rain over the past four days. After a long walk, we came upon a road that would take us to Mavis Bank Square. It was now 3:20 p.m., and we had been traveling on foot for over six and one-half hours. The only time we stopped was in the pepper field. At this point my feet ached after traveling barefooted for such a long time.

Chapter 16: The Prayer

One of the gentlemen lost one of his shoes, and he probably may not have even realized it until he reached the road because he was still wearing the one shoe. This could well be the very best pair of shoes he had. We put together whatever funds we could and paid the gentleman for showing us the way, even though he did not actually ask for any money. We spotted a Land Rover parked in a yard, and we called out to the owner, trying to get a lift to Mavis Bank Square. We were really tired and found it very difficult to continue walking. The driver felt sorry for us and was willing to take us to the square, but the owner declined our request.

The gentleman who showed us the way told us that the walk to the square would take fifteen minutes. We started walking, but soon, we were relieved of that agony as the driver, seemingly against the owner's directives, came and drove us to Mavis Bank Square. Contrary to what the gentleman told us, the drive took us approximately twenty minutes—so the walk would have been much longer. While we were in the vehicle, people were running out of their houses and looking at us as the news spread about the group that went up into the mountains and got lost.

Chapter 17

Rivers and Mountains— Our Separation from God

Our group determined in our hearts that we wanted to attend the funeral service. There were many problems, but the greatest one of all was the river that was lying between us and the funeral rendezvous. So, when we met at the river, the easiest thing to have done was to turn back. It looked hopeless at the time to cross the river because we did not know that was also the road to Halls Delight. When we later found out that it was the main road that should take us to Halls Delight, our faith was tested even more. How would we make it across the raging river? There was nothing to encourage us to cross this water. The only thing we had going for us was our determination to go to the funeral to support our friend and colleague who had lost his mother.

Chapter 17: Rivers and Mountains—Our Separation from God

In our personal lives and undoubtedly in our Christian life, there is always something that Satan tries to put between God and us. From the onset, the river looked serious, and the water was raging. The color of the water was not clear. It was brown because the water collected everything in its path. There were mud and all kinds of debris going with the flow of the river.

Sometimes the things that Satan uses as an attempt to separate us from God seem so important to us. One thing is linked to another, and we believe if we give up on one, it will affect the others. We realize just as how the river was carrying so much junk, we believe we would be losing out because if we truly want to follow Christ, we would have to give up on so much of the junk in our lives. So, we have rivers, muddy, dirty rivers that separate us from God.

Satan makes sure that this river flows every day, and it collects all the sins we have done in times past and present, and it reminds us each day of our messy situation. The water is raging as the devil tries to keep us on his side. Many times, he tries to show us that our Savior is not there. He reminds us of what we are going through and tells us that God will never hear us. Sometimes or a lot of times, we tend to believe him, as we really do not "see" our Protector. We might pray to Him, but we do not get any response, or so we thought, while the muddy and dirty water continues to flow.

There are situations in our lives that are causing a separation from our heavenly Father, but we must take the brave step, face these challenges, face these rivers, these trials, and call upon our heavenly Father to help us set sail across our river. In Romans 8:38–39, Paul declares, "For I am persuaded that neither death, nor life, nor angels, nor principalities, nor powers, nor things present, nor things to come, nor height, nor depth, nor any other creature, shall be able to separate us from the love of God, which is in Christ Jesus our Lord."

The river could be heard from miles away, but no doubt, it could not have been mistaken for anything but the river. Once the sound is heard, one would know it was the sound of the river. Sometimes we try to connect with Christ, but because we are known for the sins we do, people will scoff at us, and they will determine for us that God does not have any use for us. When they see us trying to go on the Christian journey, they will say it's only for a short time; she will soon go back to her evil ways. Our God can change the sound of our lives from the strong surging, hounding sound of the river to a peaceful, pleasant flow. He can take any ugly situation and make it pleasant. We must let go and let God clean up our riverbeds of sin so that when there is an overflow, only good things will be collected and carried in the water. People will know us by our sound and will soon forget about our dirty side and become amazed by how the Lord has blessed us and cleansed us tremendously.

Okay, so we have dirty rivers in our lives, but it does not have to end there. Let the Lord clean the river. Allow the Holy Spirit to work from the inside out and watch the blessings of the Lord flow. Yes, we will be carrying things as the river flows but not mud and garbage, but we will be proclaiming the words of God and helping to win souls for His kingdom.

The Lord has now cleansed us. We thought Satan was finished with us, but that is not the case. He works hard and tries daily to bring about a separation between God and us. We have overcome our rivers, and Satan realizes that he can no longer tempt us on these issues, so he examines us and looks for other weak spots where he can throw his fiery darts. He, therefore, places mountains in our way.

As a group, as soon as we crossed the river, we were faced with the challenges of climbing the mountains. There was no time in between.

Satan does not hesitate. As soon as we gain the victory over one sin, he brings another obstacle in our lives. We, on our own, can do nothing. We have to rely on our Father to help us. Sometimes we will ask Him to remove the mountain, and He will; sometimes we will ask Him to take us out of the mountain, and He will, but sometimes only when we struggle and reach the peak of the mountain can we see the glory of God in our lives. Only then will we have the "mountaintop experience."

So, it was rivers, then mountains, and each day there will be something else. But the same God who was with us through the rivers and mountains will be with us through our fiery trials. We can make it with Jesus, who will supply all our needs. The Lord promises to be with us even when this world scorns, ridicules, and even persecutes us.

Chapter 18

Square at Last

Merlyn's car was left unattended without any form of security. I must commend the community members as no one attempted to break into the vehicle. Angels kept guard while it was left there. Other vehicles were also parked there, and these were also not tampered with. To God be the glory! After we reached the square, Merlyn went for her car, and we sat in it at the square in our wet clothes and had the unrefrigerated cooked food that Hirfa and Merlyn brought for lunch the morning before. We also did not have any means of heating it up. We had not had any food tasting so good. Even Pastor Willis admitted to the fact. We were starving!

When we were ready to go, the car would not start as there was a battery problem. We were only thinking of the food and didn't realize that the car light was on. After getting help from the men in the area, we were able to jump-start the car and soon were on our way home. I must say that we were fortunate as we had our ride with us. The rest of the travelers, inclusive of Pastor Willis' wife, had no ready transportation because the vehicle that took them to the river left the same day. They had to find a ride to take them out of Mavis Bank, then to Kingston, where they would take another ride to the Parish of Trelawny. That should take another six to eight hours because of the weather condition. They were all soaking wet!

We were later informed that some members of the bereaved family, who came from America to attend the funeral and had advised us not to go up the mountains, had to take the same route that we did in order to catch their flight back to the US. This was due to the fact that the weather condition had not improved even days after we left.

Chapter 19

Leaving Mavis Bank

We were so happy that we had crossed the river and were heading home. We had no idea that trouble was not yet over. After driving for a while, we reached a section where the road was covered with mud. There was a landslide in the area that resulted in the roadway partially blocked with sludge. The mud was thick and we tried to pass through, but the car got stuck. We did not attempt to get out of the car but again, the Lord sent us help. A gentleman came by and told Merlyn to put the car in the lowest gear, then she should press as hard as she could on the accelerator. The car shot forward and we were out. Praise God! The people are accustomed to these situations and know how to get out of them. Merlyn drove carefully on the road, but we came to another stumbling block on Gordon Town Road in Kingston. There was another river to cross. We thought that we had crossed all the rivers. This was just too much for one day! This river was flowing heavily and swiftly across the road. It looked serious as the road was not very wide, was even breaking away at the edges, and we could be easily washed over the side. We stopped and waited—waited on the Lord for help. The same gentleman who helped us out of the mud came. It seemed that the Lord was using him to lead us out. He told Merlyn to follow behind him. I must say that Merlyn did not show any sign of fear. She is a courageous woman in and out of her car. She followed behind the car, and soon, we crossed the river and were heading home.

Even in Kingston we encountered a lot of water. One-way lanes turned into two ways as roads were flooded out. Again, I must commend Merlyn as she knew her whereabouts in Kingston and was able to navigate her way out.

> *There was another river to cross. We thought that we had crossed all the rivers. This was just too much for one day!*

While we were still driving, the ladies started to feel very uncomfortable, and loud music was now playing in their stomachs. The two-day-old food that we devoured was now taking its toll on them, and they were now searching for somewhere to have it released. Kentucky Fried Chicken's bathroom to the rescue! I was not feeling the urge, so I waited in the car while the three ladies went and relieved themselves of the discomfort. I was not accustomed to seeing my co-workers looking so disheveled—walking through the city of Kingston in their little shorts, all wet and with their hair out of place. However, their hairs were processed and would be easier to get back to normal. Mine was natural and was longer than shoulder length. I had it in a rope twist, which unraveled from the battering of the rain. I was wondering how I would get my hair styled in order to report to work the next day. I called my husband to inform him that we were in Kingston. From the sound of his voice, I knew that he was very disappointed to hear that we were only in Kingston (approximately one and one-half hours away under normal circumstances, but because of the weather, it could take up to twice the normal time) and not nearer home. For myself and the rest of the group, this was very comforting.

In our Christian walk, our heavenly Father does not promise us that we will always have a smooth path. He does not promise us that things will always be okay because Satan is like a roaring lion, seeking to devour. The Lord does not promise us a road of ease.

The journey from Halls Delight to home is a reminder that on our Christian journey, we will experience challenges. As a matter of fact, if we have it any other way, then we are in trouble. The Lord does not promise us tranquility at all times. It was not easy when he sent His only begotten Son to die in our stead. We must, therefore, through the grace of God, overcome our obstacles. God does not promise us ease, but He promises that He will take us through our difficulties. He is our Guide and Stay. In Psalm 23:4,

Chapter 19: Leaving Mavis Bank

it says, "Yea, though I walk through the valley of the shadow of death, I will fear no evil: for thou art with me; thy rod and thy staff they comfort me."

Our heavenly Father promises guidance, protection, healing, and peace of mind. Yes, He promises peace in the midst of the storm. Psalm 91:11–12 says, "For He shall give His angels charge over thee, to keep thee in all thy ways. They shall bear thee up in their hands, lest thou dash thy foot against a stone."

While we were trying to overcome our obstacles by going up in the mountains, we had many other detractors. One of these was people trying to discourage us from going forward. Some wanted us to go back to Halls Delight. In our Christian walk, there are those who are always looking for us to go back on our commitment to Christ. Satan works hard, trying to help us turn back. Just as how the people told us that it was unsafe, the devil tells us that it is no use serving God. He tells us that we are hopeless, trying to serve God.

How many times have you, as a Christian, doubted that God really hears you and that you will not make it to the kingdom? I have doubted myself many times but get comfort from the Scriptures that He did not come to call the righteous but sinners unto repentance (see Mark 2:17). Satan may tempt us to give up on God, but he does not have the power to make us do so. We, therefore, have a choice—the choice to go forward with the Lord or backward to sin and Satan. As a group, we, too, had a choice to climb the mountains in order to go home or remain in the situation that we were in. We chose the former. We should also make the choice to serve God so that we may live and reign with Him when He comes to take His children home.

There were some people who told us to remain where we were. They said we should not go forward or backward. Satan also tells us to remain in sin. He is happy when we make no effort to study the Word of God and try to obey His will. God cannot help us at this stage. We must make the decision to climb out of the mountains of sin. Only then will He go before us and lead us out safely.

Some told us not to proceed; they, however, did not have an option for us. There are so-called Christians who Satan places into the churches. These are there trying to criticize and tear down a trying Christian. If a member should make an error, they would be the ones to echo it not only in the church community but the community at large. They are not quick to pray for others but are usually self-righteous and unforgiving. They always wish for something to go wrong in order to say, "I told you so." They are quick to point out the faults of the brethren, just as how the people of the community were quick to tell us that we should not go. They do not offer any solution, and they hold on to things of the past that members might have done and make reference to them whenever they get the chance. They find pleasure in doing harm to their brothers and sisters.

Satan works in many forms, but God is still in the lead, and He has promised that if we are willing, He will guide us safely through. Just as we lost a part of our clothing, not everybody will come through in one piece when they decide to serve God. Some will lose their lives; others will lose limbs, their health, homes, or family members, during their walk with God. In Matthew 24:13, Jesus said, "But he that shall endure unto the end, the same shall be saved." So, we need not worry because whatever was lost will be regained when Christ comes to take us home. The blind will see, and the deaf will hear; as a matter of fact, those who die in the Lord will rise to an incorruptible body. Those who are alive will also be transformed, and we shall see Jesus as He is—the One who died for our sins and whom we have waited for so long. In Job 19:26–27, it says, "And after my skin is destroyed, this I know, that in my flesh I shall see God, whom I shall see for myself, and my eyes shall behold, and not another."

Second Timothy 2:11–12 says, "It is a faithful saying: For if we be dead with Him, we shall live with Him: If we suffer, we shall also reign with Him."

The group of us remained faithful by climbing the mountains and crossing the rivers just to be home with our families. The Lord God kept us safe, and even though we were in the sometimes-pelting rain for almost two days, none of us from the group of four got sick later on. We did not even get the common cold or flu. Thanks be to God!

Chapter 19: Leaving Mavis Bank

The energy that we had to get home should be the very same we have to work through the instilling of the Holy Spirit so that we make it into the kingdom of God. This energy must be exercised by studying God's Word, living a life of faithfulness and obedience to Him, and witnessing to others. If we can display such energy as we did back then, we can accomplish greater work for the Lord in our part of the vineyard.

Chapter 20

Angels—Our Special Silent Guides

God is interested in every person individually. Every child that is born has an accompanying angel, a guardian angel, who keeps the heavenly Father informed concerning his progress. During the person's lifetime, this angel does everything possible to protect and draw him or her to Christ. He will never leave them when they are tempted and makes every effort to keep them from falling prey to the enemy who would destroy his or her soul. As long as there is hope until they resist the Holy Spirit to their eternal ruin, they will be guarded by this silent, invisible companion. They will never walk alone! Even in the closing scenes of life, this guardian angel will be with them. This angel never slumbers nor sleeps and is ever present to deliver. (*Angels: We Never Walk Alone,* p. 58)

Each of us had our guardian angels who kept watch over us during our entire ordeal. They helped us to cross the river. If our eyes were opened to see heavenly beings, we would have seen how Satan tried to have the truck washed away in the river. But our guardian angels stayed with us. We would have seen how much the angels had to keep guard while we traveled to Halls Delight in the truck. So many things could have gone wrong during our entire journey, but the angels protected our every move.

Our angels protected us as we traveled back home. We climbed the mountain ... angels were there. The river was below us while we climbed the mountain, and if there were any slippage and fall, we would have gone in the river ... angels were there holding us

Chapter 20: Angels—Our Special Silent Guides

up. Even though the earth was saturated by the continuous rainfall, angels went before us, and they cut and cleared the path for us. We were protected by our angels until we were safely through. They are always with us, and that is why we should be careful what we do or say because they take back a report to our heavenly Father of the things that we do.

Sometimes as Christians, we do wrong, we go places we have no business, and enter grounds where the holy angels cannot go with us. Why should we do that? We do it mostly when we want to satisfy self. If our eyes were to be opened, we would realize the struggles the angels go through trying to keep Satan and his demons from destroying our lives. We would then not go to the clubs because we know the angels will not be there; we would not have sex before marriage because angels are keeping watch. We would not tell lies, steal, backbite, envy, covet, murder with our tongues because we know that angels are recording our actions.

We must thank God for His protection over us and for giving His angels "charge over thee, to keep thee in all thy ways. They shall bear thee up in their hands, lest thou dash thy foot against a stone" (Ps. 91:11–12, KJV). If we know that the angels take back reports to heaven, then even our every conversation would be holy. We must always be mindful that our angels are always here to protect us. Our angels are here to walk with us, to hold us up when we fall by the wayside, to give us encouragement on our Christian journey, to help minister to our every need. What a mighty and compassionate God we serve!

Chapter 21

In One Accord

It would have been so difficult if we were not in agreement on every issue as it relates to us crossing the river in order to go home. The outcome would have been so different. Our heavenly Father would not be able to work through us and lead us home as He is not the author of confusion. Instead of bickering and complaining, we stayed together, and whatever decisions were made, were made by everyone as we had one common goal of trying to get to our homes.

Unlike the children of Israel, our minds were not set on where we were coming from. We did not murmur about what we left back at Halls Delight. The children of Israel were ungrateful, and each miracle they witnessed should have helped them to overcome the next trial. They, however, were not united, and because of this, they allowed Satan to put doubts in their minds. They often forgot about what God did for them and quickly went into the path of the destroyer. God's wrath was kindled so many times against the Israelites, yet because of His mercy, He continued to provide for them.

In the book of Acts, the disciples were in the upper room tarrying for the Holy Spirit, and He was poured out only when they were in one accord. They were able on the day of Pentecost to speak in tongues so that everybody could have heard and understood the gospel of Jesus in their own language. Because of the unity, Christ added to the church three thousand souls in one day.

If the church today were united, much more would be accomplished for Christ. If we were our brothers' keepers, we would know when our brother is hungry, and we would see when he is naked. Instead of talking about the brother, we would bless him with good gifts.

Chapter 21: In One Accord

When we are united in every aspect and on all issues, then we will see the out-pouring of the Holy Spirit, and many souls will then be drawn to the kingdom of God.

> *If the church today were united, much more would be accomplished for Christ.*

Noah and his family obeyed God, and in unity and amidst ridicule, criticism, and scorn, each member played his or her part and helped to build the ark. They must have faced discouragements, but they were united in their efforts. The Bible did not say that there were discouragements coming from within the family. Because of the unity and the great faith they had in God, they were able to overcome all negativity. They stuck together even though Noah's children were adults and married, they obeyed their father and ultimately God.

When unity is evident, greatness can be accomplished. When we are in one accord, the activities of the church will run smoothly and effectively, and the pastor and elders and just a few members will not be seen as the only ones to do evangelism.

When we are in one accord, we will have interest in even the physical building of the church. We will not deface the church building in any way. We will take care of church equipment and ensure that our children do likewise. We will contribute to its upkeep and make sure that the same interest we have in keeping our homes clean and beautiful will be the same attentiveness we have for the church. We would support all programs irrespective of who is leading out. We will attend not only divine worship but Sabbath School, AYM (Adventist Youth Ministry), and Wednesday night prayer meetings. When we are in one accord, instead of calling our friends to gossip, we would call them to pray and to give words of encouragement to those who are weak and feeble. When we are in one accord, we would cry with those who are sad, hurt with those who are hurting, celebrate with those who are successful.

When we are in one accord, no member in the church would be in need. We would look out for one another and ensure that each one's needs are being met.

When we are in one accord, there will be an out-pouring of the Holy Spirit, and Jesus will be seen and felt, and many will be running to the church daily.

In one accord means that just as the body depends on each member to function effectively, we should depend on each other to be effectual witnesses for Christ. Oh, how beautiful it would be to see brethren living together in love and unity.

The group of us were in one accord. Even though we made poor decisions, we did not cast blame on each other. We trusted God and worked together. None of us had negative comments. We worked together until we crossed the river by going up into the mountains.

As a group, we stayed together, we slept together, we prayed together, we ate together. We did not have much to eat, but we were very thankful for the little we had, and the Lord blessed us immensely. We had food to eat that was not in a refrigerator for two days, yet none of us got sick. The Lord protected us in that situation. Everyone was in agreement, and this unity brought about strength, and with strength came determination, and with determination came success. To God be the glory!

Chapter 22

Home, Here We Come

Very soon, we were entering Sligoville as the other two main roads, Barry and the Bog Walk Gorge, were impassable. Bog Walk Gorge was the main road from Kingston to Ocho Rios at that time, and the two other roads, Barry and Sligoville, were alternative routes. It was my first time traveling on this road. I always heard how long the journey is through Sligoville. It was indeed a long journey. I looked, peeped, and waited anxiously just to see the main road again. I kept asking, "Are we near to the main?" This line, I believe, must at times have been extremely painful to Merlyn's ears, but I could not help it. The journey seemed forever. After a long drive, we were back on the main road to Ocho Rios.

We arrived in Ocho Rios at approximately 7:00 p.m. I felt at home. We dropped off Veneice at the square in Ocho Rios and headed for Salem—a journey that would take us approximately thirty minutes, but because of the weather, it took us approximately forty-five minutes. I called my husband, and he picked me up in Salem—a few minutes from home.

We are on the final stretch toward our heavenly home, and the holy city is almost in view. When Jesus left this earth, He told His disciples to go preach and teach, baptizing in the name of the Father and the Son and the Holy Ghost. This is what we should be doing now. The energy we had trying to go back home should now be doubled working for our Master in an effort to try and win as many souls as possible for the heavenly kingdom.

We know that Christ is gone to prepare a place for us, and we know that He is coming back for us. In this new home, there will be no night there, for Jesus will be our light. Home where the lion and leopards will play; home where there will be peace forevermore—that's the home we want to go to.

Like all the trials we went through when we were going home from Halls Delight, we will meet upon even more obstacles and tests and may even be persecuted but, "Blessed are those who are persecuted for righteousness's sake: for theirs the kingdom of heaven" (Matt. 5:10). The Bible says that in the last days, perilous times will come (see 2 Tim. 3:1). We, however, do not have to fear because God does not give us the spirit of fear but of power, and of love, and of a sound mind (see 2 Tim. 1:7). We should boldly proclaim the gospel of Christ. Yes, we are nearing home. We are on the home stretch, so we must stay prepared to meet our maker.

We must get busy for the Master and spread the gospel of Christ. In order to do this, we have to be in constant communion with God through prayer and fasting. In everything that we want to do, we first should first seek guidance from our Heavenly Father and allow the Holy Spirit to lead us. He should also guide our thoughts because these deliberations become actions. When we live by the Word of God, then His character will be reflected in our lives. Only a Christ-like character will take us to heaven. Our lifestyles must be a living testimony to the world so we, therefore, should not crave for the things of the world. Because we are in the world but not of this world, less time should be spent on the things that keep us from God, such as the watching of the soaps and the Lifetime movies. This will allow for more time to be spent in prayer and supplication and the engagement in personal and evangelistic outreach.

Each new day reminds us that we are closer to our God. Prayer is the key that unlocks heaven's door. We should not only pray for ourselves but also we should constantly put our children, our families, our friends, neighbors, and even our enemies before the throne of grace. There are so many things to distract people from serving God wholeheartedly. Satan does not cease but finds every way possible to try and thwart the minds of many, both young and old. If a believer should leave the ark of safety, we should not cease praying for him or her until he or she returns to the fold. Prayer moves mountains, and even the stubborn heart can be melted if prayed for earnestly.

When we are connected to God through prayer, we will see the need to read His words. His Word is truth. It is a lamp unto my feet and a light unto my path (see Ps. 119:105). We read His words and hide them in our hearts so we will know more about Him and effectively witness to others of His goodness. We must fortify our minds with the Word of God so that when our faith is tested, we will be able to deliver. Job's faith was tested, but he overcame because of his constant praying and close relationship with God, and his obedience to Him. He did not yield, not even to his wife's suggestion to curse God and die. He could not have done that because he had the character of Christ. The three Hebrew boys (even when threatened with the fiery furnace) also stood up to the test and did not bow when they were demanded to bow to the image.

Because of envy and jealousy, Joseph's brothers, after an attempt to have him killed, sold him into slavery. In all this Joseph still trusted God. He did not see the way out. He did not see any sense in the situation. He did not know why his God would allow such terrible ordeal to overtake him, but he remained faithful. When Potiphar's wife made a pass at him, he did not think about the consequences she would bring on him if he declined her wishes. He thought about the consequences if he sinned, so he asked the question, how could I do such a thing and sin against my God? Because of the stance he took, Joseph was brought low and placed in prison for a crime he did not commit, but in God's time, he was released and promoted to second in command to Pharoah.

We must read the Word of God for ourselves because there is going to come a time when we will not have the Bible to read, and we will have to go off what we have implanted in our minds. How sad it will be if, at the end of it all, we are not able to go by the Word because all this time, we were just playing church and not cementing the Word in our minds.

Brothers and sisters, let us read God's Word. Let us find time to study them. The end is nearer than we believe; it is even at the door. We should, therefore, not be engaged in idle conversations;

our minds must be tuned heavenward. When we have a healthy prayer life and know the Scriptures for ourselves, then we will have a burning desire to witness for our Master.

> *Jesus should be seen in all our conversations.*

After we have a prayed-up life and have been studying the Word of God, we must go out and tell others of the coming of our Savior. This good news should be told to whomever we come in contact with. There should be a burning desire to tell. We should live Christ, and those looking at us should see that there is something different about us. People should want to have the Jesus we have, and we should help them find Him. We should not be the ones to complain about the trials we are going through and about the economic hardships. We should use these as testimonies as to how our God has provided for us throughout these hard times. Jesus should be seen in all our conversations and our dealings with everyone, and everywhere we go.

Chapter 23

Home in View

As the road signs to Ocho Rios reminded us that we were nearing home, we are now seeing signs that tell us that we are nearing our heavenly home. One songwriter said that we should look for the way-marks, the prophetic way-marks. The Bible said in the end time there will be wars and rumors of wars, there will be famines and earthquakes in diverse places. We have seen so many wars taking place, and these are happening in places where we have never seen them before.

People are scared for their lives because of terrorism. Even within our own countries where we live, there is terrorism. Domestic terrorism is on the increase. Bullying in the schools is on the rise and so are the incidents of school shootings. Children are sent to school and are murdered there. What kind of world are we living in? This is one sign. Yes! These are definite waymarks telling us that the coming of the Lord is near.

We live in a world where we have to be scared for our children. Children have to be under close watch at all times because predators and sex offenders are lying in wait to snatch them away. Every chance they get to take away a child, they do so. Children are going missing, teenagers are going missing, adults are going missing. The hearts of men are desperately wicked.

Divorce is on the rise because people harden the hearts and refuse to reconcile. Many did not marry for the right reasons in the first place. The Bible says that as it was in Noah's day, so it will be today. Many will be marrying and given in marriage. Husbands are abusing wives, and wives abusing husbands. Couples are trying to solve their problems and are not finding time to pray and turning everything over to Jesus. This is the time we live in.

Mothers are sleeping with their daughter's lovers, and daughters are doing the very same to their mothers. Sisters are fighting over the same lover and are even having children for the same man. Fathers and mothers are sleeping with their children. Teenagers are having children. Yes, these are signs that Christ's coming is near.

The economy is in shambles. Yes, the US lost AAA rating in 2011! One party is blaming the other for the mess that we are in. All over the world, countries are in financial turmoil. Money will soon have no value.

People are losing their jobs, homeowners are losing their homes, and homelessness is increasing. We see countries in economic and political unrest. We are witnessing more hate crimes by extremists, and we also have an increase in police brutality. We see people calling wrong right and right wrong. We do not have any confidence in the political parties, and in many cases, they have not stood up for the rights of minorities. The Scripture tells us that when we see these signs, we should look up for our redemption draweth nigh (see Luke 21:28).

Natural disasters are an almost everyday affair. Tornadoes, earthquakes, tsunamis, fires, floods, and droughts are evidences of climate change. There are many man-made disasters as well. People are leading lifestyles that only lead to self-destruction. Rich people are still unhappy and many struggle with mental illnesses. Oh, Lord, sometimes it seems as if You are not in control. When we see these things, sometimes, we tend to question and become doubtful about your existence. Where are You in all this? Where is Your mercy?

Many people are dying by gun violence. Others are dying from numerous sicknesses and diseases. The COVID-19 pandemic has claimed the lives of over six hundred thousand in the USA and over four million worldwide. Abuse of women, children, and minorities, along with starvation continue to take their toll on the human population. The things are happening, but the scripture is clear that the end is still not yet. There is worse yet to come? Lord we need you to come quickly to take your people home.

Chapter 23: Home in View

DOES JESUS CARE?

Each morning I wake and listen to the newscast,
I wonder what is happening; things are just happening too fast.
Each day I hear not one or two, but "many are dead!"
And the usual saying that "earth a run red!"

Some people tend to question God on the country's negative image
Some say that Satan has controlled the earth and is on a rampage
Others have no comments but sense something is wrong,
But all want a solution to the senseless killing. Oh, man!

One thing I want to ask, does Jesus really care?
Each day loved ones are missing, so many we loved so dear,
The senseless everyday killings, my God, this is not fair!
I just wonder, I just ask this question, does Jesus really care?

Does Jesus care when a child is abused?
When the mother stays aside and allows the child to be used,
When a child is taken out of school and has to go find work,
Because his daddy is really, really a big jerk.

Does Jesus care when church members are suffering really hard?
They are without jobs because they keep the commands of God.
But worst when they are oppressed by their own church brethren,
Should they be strong in God and heed to His calling?

Does Jesus care when the one child you have dies?
When the child decides to take up the gun because in it he confides,
When the children are turning away from the church they were raised in,
When to them, everything is okay and wrong actions not seen as a sin,

Does Jesus care when the wife is abused by the man?

And she is forced to stay home and subject herself to his action.
When the father is killed by the son or the mother by the daughter,
Oh, I feel the pain; there is no space for laughter.

Does Jesus care when sickness creeps in?
Asthma, cancer, heart condition, lupus, HIV/AIDS, corona virus, because of this terrible sin,
When people from all walks of life are crying each and every day,
Tell me the truth, can we really tell them that to our God they can pray?

Does Jesus care? Oh, so many children having children?
No regard for the Word of God, yes, this is the time we live in,
Does Jesus care? Oh, my heart is so sad,
As the news keeps coming each day, and things are getting very, very bad.

Mother living with daughter's spouse, oh stop, please!
The low regard for marriage is on the increase!
A world where many wrongdoings are allowed.
What has this world gone to? God, I need to hear You clear and loud!

I sat there quietly, patiently, waiting for the Lord to respond,
I opened up my heart to God; I held on to His unchanging hand,
Then the Holy Spirit said to me, even though it seemed the world is a disaster,
Jesus really cares, He loves you, and to this mess, He is the only answer.

I started reflecting on my own life,
I, too, at times, have experienced misery and strife,
When it seemed that everything was crushing in, it is so dark I can't see!
When there was no light at the tunnel, Jesus shone His light on me.

Chapter 23: Home in View

Just like the woman with the issue of blood who waited for years,
To be relieved of her sickness, the pain brought her many tears,
But when she touched Jesus, instantly she was healed,
And as to how much Jesus cares? This was again revealed.

Job was sick unto death, but with God, he stayed,
Condition kept worsening but more so to God Job prayed,
He too could have cursed God; sometimes he must have felt much fear.
But faith can move mountain; Job found out Jesus really cares.

My Jesus cares when all seems but lost.
When so many are dying and are going senselessly to the dust,
That is why He sends us to take to the world this great commission,
To tell the dying souls of His great salvation.

O yes, He cares, I know He cares!
His heart is touched with my grief and your grief,
Let us, therefore, give a helping hand to our fallen sister and brother,
And help to guide them in the right path, their burdens can be relieved.

Does Jesus Care, O yes, He cares. He is our Savior and Lord!
Let us, therefore, take this news of hope all over this world.
By: Carline Samuels

As Christians, what should we do? What must we do? We cannot sit on the sidelines neither can we sit idly by. We cannot be afraid. We have to point the lost to Christ. If we do not do this, how can we make it to the kingdom? We cannot go to heaven with a starless crown. We have to work because we know that the night is coming.

We cannot be afraid, my brothers and sisters. We have to comfort and encourage one another. We must know that all things work together for good to those who love the Lord. When we are faced with disappointments, we must trust God for the right outcome. Let us hold fast to the profession of our faith. We are nearing home, and we are now seeing signs. The way-marks are clear, and with every new day, it means we are closer to the Lord's coming.

We see today people scoffing at the Word of God. They are asking where is God? The gospel has been proclaimed; ever since they were a child they have been hearing about Christ's coming, and today, nothing has happened. Just like the children of Israel, when they crossed over the promised land and after many generations were passed, these Israelites turned to idolatry. They were serving gods other than the God who delivered their forefathers. So, it is today. We have a lot of scoffers. People do not want to use the Bible as their guide. Everybody has their own interpretation of the Scriptures and does not want to rely on the Holy Spirit to interpret and guide them into truth. Many have itching ears and will believe any fallible that will fit into their lifestyles. But the Scriptures say woe unto the unjust when Christ puts in His appearance. It will be joy for the righteous, but for the unrighteous, it would have been better if they were not born. The only way we will not get detracted by these scoffers is if we study the Word of God.

> The Lord is not slack concerning his promise, as some men count slackness; but is longsuffering to us-ward, not willing that any should perish, but that all should come to repentance. But the day of the Lord will come as a thief in the night; in the which the heavens shall pass away with a great noise, and the elements shall melt with fervent heat, the earth also and the works that are therein shall be burned up. (2 Peter 3:9–10)

Satan mixes truth with error, and if we do not know the Word, we will be deceived. Satan tried to deceive Jesus when he was tempting Him after the fast. He used the very scriptures to tempt Him, but because Jesus is the Word, He was able to overcome by using the scriptures: "It is written." Eve, too, was tempted to doubt God, but sad to say, Eve yielded to this temptation. We have to be fortified to the Word of God in order not to be deceived by the tempter.

In these end times, there will be many anti-Christ proclaiming to be the messiah. The scripture says that if we hear that he is in the desert, we should not go there. If we believe the Scriptures, we should be very careful not to listen or follow anyone who says or does anything that is contrary. We should avoid attending any such services, workshops, and seminars that go against the Word of God, as when we do that, we are going into areas where the angels will not go with us. We have to be very careful of where we go and what we listen to. We should also be careful of even the very words we sing. Sometimes the songs may sound very good as the beat and the rhythm are catching and pleasant, but if we take time to examine the words, we would be surprised to know what is being said.

> ***Satan mixes truth with error, and if we do not know the Word, we will be deceived.***

In these end times, we have evildoers and backbiters. Yes, these are also way-marks. Many people do not need a reason to hate, and even those you are helping will hate you. You might be doing good to someone, and they use this to covet and hate. People will behave as if they are friends and that they are close to you, but Sister White says that these are the very ones who will give us up to the authorities when the time comes. Yes, people will hate you because you are active in the church and because you are trying to live uprightly. As a matter of fact, Jesus Christ lived a righteous life on earth, yet He was accused, rejected, and eventually killed. But praise the Lord, death could not hold Him in, so on the third day, He rose triumphantly to save.

The scriptures said that we are also going to be hated and despised by many, but the scriptures also remind us to do good to our enemies. In Matthew 5:44–45, it says,

> But I say unto you, love your enemies, bless them that curse you, do good to them that hate you, and pray for

them which despitefully use you, and persecute you; That ye may be the children of your Father which is in heaven: for he maketh his sun to rise on the evil and on the good, and sendeth rain on the just and on the unjust.

We should never stumble because of the way we are treated by other church members. When we are oppressed and lied about, we should give God the glory.

We must not harbor hatred in our hearts for those who are doing bad to us, but we should pray for them. Hatred is of the devil. We should always pray for the Lord to bless our enemies and that they will see their faults and turn around before it is too late. We must pray for prosperity for them at all times. Sometimes when people are guilty, they behave as the innocent and will try to cause strife, but if the sincere Christian puts the situation before the throne of God, the Lord will bring about a favorable solution.

All we need to do is keep connected to the Lord, and He will fight our battles for us. The scripture in Proverb 16:7 says that if our ways please the Lord, then He will make our enemies be at peace with us. These are all waymarks. We have to study the Word of God and know that these are just signaling the end. We have to know that Satan will use anyone he can to do his work. While we pray for our enemies, we must pray and ask the Lord to help us that we will not fall prey to Satan and his evil devices.

Another waymark is that of the technological age that we live in. Every kind of information is just at our fingertips. What was hidden from the wise and prudent is now been revealed to the babes and sucklings. Children are being exposed to pornography at an early stage. They do not have to go far to see this as it is in the house on the television shows, in magazines, and on the Internet. Some are able to access this through cable and satellite networks as their parents have these and do not put the necessary steps in place to restrain the children from accessing them. These are destroying the minds of our children, many of whom are engaging in sexual activities at very tender ages. Parents do not have the time to monitor their children as they have to be working hard, hustling, and bustling to put food on the table and

Chapter 23: Home in View

a roof over the heads of their families. It is very disturbing to see the number of single parents, and with this kind of setting, there is no family time.

Children are sometimes left on their own to raise themselves. They feed their minds on these inappropriate media. After a while, they start to act out what they have been seeing and soon become a menace to society. Families do not eat together anymore, they do not have family worship, and the children are not taught the ways of the Lord. Moreover, the Bible has been taken out of our schools so children have one less reference point to their moral and spiritual well-being. Another sign is the dangerous foods that we eat. Manufacturers are no longer careful of how food and other supplies are being manufactured. Sometimes they go through very dangerous processes, and ingredients are used that are not fit for human consumption. They do this, however, for their own interest to speed up manufacturing time, enhance tastes that are addictive, and also to preserve the shelf life of these products. As a result, much harm is being done to the health of the consumer while the manufacturers reap huge profits. Many sicknesses and diseases, including cancers, are the result of the consumption of harmful foods. Even baby foods are not spared as the dangerous poison arsenic is found in infant juices and other foods. Because of greed, man will go to the extreme to put more money in his pocket, and this is at the expense of people's lives.

It seems that the mind is getting so immune to the situation of people dying tragically and in such large numbers that it does not have the same effect it would have some years ago. Hundreds of thousands are dying by earthquakes, floods, fires, plane crashes, tornadoes, and other disasters. These disasters are so frequent, yet some people are not alarmed. They do not realize the end is near. Sometimes only when the situation is near to us that we are called to mind what is really happening in this world. We are so caught up in acquiring material things that we are deadened to the situation.

We find time to work and work and overwork our bodies, and in so doing, we find less and less time for God. We do not pray as we should. We do not study the Scriptures as we used to. As soon as we pick up the Bible or go to our knees for prayer we get sleepy. As soon as we go on our knees to pray, sleep overtakes us. We do not get sleepy when we are engaged in other activities like watching television. The enemy is fighting really hard to keep our minds off Jesus, and His soon return. The waymarks are all over. Signs of the times are everywhere. We need to keep our eyes upon the eastern sky because we know that our redemption draws to a close.

There is so much irreverence in the church today. People do not have the respect for God anymore. If they had, the worship services would be more enriching, not "a bedlam of noise" and confusion. Things would be done in an orderly manner, and God would be given the praise He rightly deserves. If people really were to worship, then there would not be the blatant chewing of gum, texting, talking, and socializing while services are being held. It is amazing to see the level of irreverence that takes place in the house of God. Church today is like a marketplace. In a marketplace, everything takes place at once. People will even sit in the choir loft and text. This texting does not have anything to do with what is happening in church.

The attire is another waymark. Some feel that they are in competition to see who can wear the shortest and tightest, and they are seen up front, taking part in church services. People want to live any kind of life throughout the week, but on Sabbath morning, they are so bold as to approach God's throne in their inappropriate attire. We are not consumed because of the abundant mercies of our heavenly Father. Thank You, Jehovah! Back in Bible times, the priest in the sanctuary had to ensure that all of his sins were forgiven before he could enter into the Most Holy Place to minister on behalf of the people. If all sins were not forgiven, he surely would drop dead. Why don't we drop dead when we go barefacedly before God to do business on His behalf? Why don't we drop dead when we know we are having sex out of marriage, when we cheat on our spouses, when we tell lies, steal, covet, envy? Why don't we drop dead? The reason is because of the grace of God. We know once we go to Him with sincerity of heart, He will forgive our sins.

Chapter 23: Home in View

We, therefore, sin continuously as we know God will forgive our sins.

But the Lord will not always be there when we call on Him for forgiveness of sins. The Holy Spirit will leave us eventually after we continue to reject Him. What shall we do, shall we continue in sin so that grace may abound? God forbid! We should ask God to help us to humble ourselves, and try to live a life that is pleasing to our God.

Whatever the Lord says, Satan says the opposite. In the Garden of Eden, God said that if Adam and his wife ate the fruit, they would surely die. Satan said, "You shall not surely die." God said a man shall take a woman, and they shall become one flesh. Satan says a man can take many women and also sanction other forms of marriages. God says remember the Sabbath day to keep it holy. Satan says any other day is good enough. The Bible teaches marriage before sex; Satan says sex before marriage.

Satan also counterfeits the Sabbath of the Lord. In Exodus 20:8–11 the scriptures say, "Remember the sabbath day to keep it holy." Satan says any day. In the creation week, God did all His work in six literal days. He rested on the seventh day and commanded us do likewise. We keep the Sabbath of the Lord our God because we are in obedience to His Word. Christ said that "If you love me, keep my commandments" (John 14:15). If we break one, we are guilty of all, so, therefore, we keep the fourth. Many will say that the fourth is done away with, but in Hebrews 4:8–9, the scripture says, "For if Jesus had given them rest, then would he not afterward have spoken of another day. There remaineth therefore a rest to the people of God." There is also no evidence in Scripture to show that the Sabbath was done away with. The seven-day cycle has not been broken, therefore, even though men tampered with the calendar, the seven-day week has not changed. The scriptures says in James 2:10–12:

> For whosoever shall keep the whole law, and yet offend in one point, he is guilty of all. For he that said, Do not commit adultery, said also, Do not kill. Now if thou commit no adultery, yet if thou kill, thou art become a transgressor

of the law. So speak ye, and so do, as they that shall be judged by the law of liberty.

One of the biggest counterfeits Satan has today is the Creation story. Through evolution, men have given their own explanation for the origin of the world and how mankind came into existence. This is one of the biggest theories that is even taught in the public schools, and students who do not believe this story are required to do the studies. Let us take a look at the Creation account. Let us look at the entire chapter of Genesis 1.

> In the beginning God created the heaven and the earth. And the earth was without form, and void; and darkness was upon the face of the deep. And the spirit of God moved upon the face of the waters. And God said, Let there be light: and there was light. And God saw the light, that it was good: and God divided the light from the darkness. And God called the light Day, and the darkness he called Night. And the evening and the morning were the first day. And God said, Let there be a firmament in the midst of the waters, and let it divide the waters from the waters. And God made the firmament, and divided the waters which were under the firmament from the waters which were above the firmament: and it was so. And God called the firmament Heaven. And the evening and the morning were the second day. And God said, Let the waters under the heaven be gathered together unto one place, and let the dry land appear: and it was so. And God called the dry land Earth; and the gathering together of the waters called he Seas: and God saw that it was good. And God said, Let the earth bring forth grass, the herb yielding seed, and the fruit tree yielding fruit after his kind, whose seed is in itself, upon the earth: and it was so. And the earth brought forth grass, and herb yielding seed after his kind, and the tree yielding fruit, whose seed was in itself, after his kind: and God saw that it was good. And the evening and the morning were the third day. And God said, Let there be lights in the firmament of the heaven to

divide the day from the night; and let them be for signs, and for seasons, and for days, and years; And let them be for lights in the firmament of the heaven to give light upon the earth: and it was so. And God made two great lights; the greater light to rule the day, and the lesser light to rule the night: he made the stars also. And God set them in the firmament of the heaven to give light upon the earth, And to rule over the day and over the night, and to divide the light from the darkness: and God saw that it was good. And the evening and the morning were the fourth day. And God said, Let the waters bring forth abundantly the moving creature that hath life, and fowl that may fly above the earth in the open firmament of heaven. And God created great whales, and every living creature that moveth, which the waters brought forth abundantly, after their kind, and every winged fowl after his kind: and God saw that it was good. And God blessed them, saying, Be fruitful, and multiply, and fill the waters in the seas, and let fowl multiply in the earth. And the evening and the morning were the fifth day. And God said, Let the earth bring forth the living creature after his kind, cattle, and creeping thing, and beast of the earth after his kind: and it was so. And God made the beast of the earth after his kind, and cattle after their kind, and every thing that creepeth upon the earth after his kind: and God saw that it was good. And God said, Let us make man in our image, after our likeness: and let them have dominion over the fish of the sea, and over the fowl of the air, and over the cattle, and over all the earth, and over every creeping thing that creepeth upon the earth. So God created man in his own image, in the image of God created he him; male and female created he them. And God blessed them, and God said unto them, Be fruitful and multiply, and replenish the earth, and subdue it: and have dominion over the fish of the sea, and over the fowl of the air, and over every living thing that moveth upon the earth. And God said, Behold, I have given you every herb bearing seed, which is upon the face of all the earth, and every tree, in the which is the fruit of a tree yielding seed; to you it shall be for meat. And to every beast of the earth, and to every fowl of the air, and to every thing that creepeth upon the earth, wherein there is life, I have given every green herb for meat: and it was so. And God saw every thing that he had made, and, behold, it was very good. And the evening and the morning were the sixth day (Gen 1:1–31). Thus the heavens and the earth were finished, and all the host of them (Gen. 2:1).

This is clear evidence in detail that God has indeed created this world, and the evolution theory cannot stand up to this.

Spiritism is on the rise in these last days. Spiritism is the belief that the living can communicate with the dead. The Bible says that the dead know nothing. Once a person dies, that very day, his thoughts perish. Just like how Mrs. Willis was afraid of water—if she were aware of what was happening at her funeral, she would have done something about it. The dead know nothing. Satan and his evil angels disguise themselves as loved ones who have died and appear to grieving family members. Members are, therefore, convinced that these are their loved ones reappearing to them. We must be reminded that we are made a little lower than the angels; therefore, we are no match for the devil.

> *Spiritism is on the rise in these last days.*

We see spiritism in movies, cartoons, and almost everything we watch on the television. Satan is using the media to slowly impart this idea in our minds. Many people believe that once a person dies, he or she goes to heaven and is looking down on the earth. When a person dies, the body returns to the ground, and the breath returns to God. There is no body returning to heaven; therefore, the deceased cannot be in heaven looking down or in another world, looking at what is taking place on earth. We sleep in our graves, and at the first trump of God, those who sleep in Him will be raised to an incorruptible body (see 1 Cor. 15:52–53). Not before. Blessed are the dead who die in the Lord (see Rev. 14:13). Blessed be the name of the Lord! He has given us through His words everything we need in order to be saved. When we have dreams of our loved ones trying to communicate with us, it is of the devil. The devil and his angels were kicked out of heaven, and the Bible said woe unto the inhabitants of the earth.

When we study the Word of God and go against what we know, the Lord is going to hold us accountable. We must teach these things to our children, when they lie down and when they wake up. Every conversation we have with them should point them heavenward. We should use every opportunity to buy religious gifts that will edify them and cut out on buying so many of the electronic games and other toys that are only teaching them violence. If we really and truly love our children, we will teach them the way of the Lord.

Children must be taught at an early age how to reverence God and how to act in the house of the Lord. If this is done, children will know how to act when they go into the sanctuary and even at home. Sister White said that children must be taught to be quiet at home. When this is done, they will reflect the same behavior pattern when they go out. She said that a quiet child at home does not mean that the child is unhappy.

Just before Jesus returns, Christians will be persecuted. We will be deprived of the Word of God. We will be tested on the issue of the Sabbath. Our faith will be tested, and we will have to know who we stand for. We have to be certain and purpose in our minds from now whom we stand for.

When we stand for Jesus, we will not be afraid to spread the gospel. When we know who we stand for, we will visit the prisons and minister to the inmates. The scripture says in Matthew 25:43, "I was in prison, and you visited me not." We will bring the message of hope to those who are incarcerated, pointing them to Jesus Christ.

The gospel is for everyone and anyone who is interested, and it is by choice. Sometimes we tend to write off murderers, drug addicts, sex offenders, and rapists, but the gospel is for them as it is for everyone else. We must, therefore, proclaim the hope of salvation to these fallen brothers and sisters. When we realize that

Satan is the mastermind behind all atrocities, then we will work with more earnestness, trying to win souls for the kingdom. We will, therefore, not be picky, but we will introduce Christ at every opportunity we get.

When we know who we stand for, we will readily and not grudgingly return our tithes and offerings. We will unhesitatingly give to other special offerings like 13th Sabbath Offerings. These offerings we know assist in various countries to set up churches and to spread the gospel of salvation to those who have never heard.

When we know who we stand for, then we will be willing to support our community outreach centers that are operating in our churches. We will not just give what we do not want, but we would give good gifts. We will budget for this, as we do our rent and mortgages and food, and will spend time going to the stores to acquire these much-needed items.

When we know who we stand for, we will allow our children to attend our church schools. We will want them to learn more about God. Education is more than just a course of study. We will want the best for our children and will seek every opportunity to steer them in the path of righteousness. Those who do not have children will see the need to assist by sponsoring a child or giving toward scholarship funds. There is a work for everyone to do.

When we know who we stand for, we will use our God-given talents to praise and glorify our Creator. We will not take the credit for ourselves. If it were left to us alone, we would not be able to utter one word, sing one note; we would not be able to think one thought, to see one glimpse of light. The Lord has given each person at least one gift. Let us not just sit on our gift but use it to proclaim God's words.

Brothers and sisters, use your gifts for the Lord. Those who can sing—sing, those who can teach—teach, those who can preach—preach, those who can prophesy—prophesy. When we do this, we would see Christ high and lifted up and many souls running to the ark of safety.

The group of us knew what we were standing for. We knew where we wanted to go. We did not know our route out of Halls

Delight, but because we were convinced that home is where we wanted to go, we took the stance and proceeded. The end result brought about success.

I encourage you, therefore, to keep your eyes on Jesus. We should engage ourselves only in holy conversations. We should refrain from speaking our own words. We should only speak a thus saith the Lord. We should not gossip but use the opportunity to sing praises to God and to lead some lost souls to Jesus Christ as we view these waymarks.

Chapter 24

Revival and Reformation

We were so happy that we were on our way home. We were out of danger and could really breathe a sigh of relief. My mind was constantly on my family back home, and with each and every mile traveled, I was happy and thankful I made it through. I felt so revived and refreshed after going through all that trial. I was strengthened both physically and emotionally. It seemed I was imagining the laughter of my husband and children. I envisioned their faces as they greeted me at the door. The very thought rejuvenated me. All that walk, all the struggles I had gone through went away from my mind. I was nearing home, and I was longing to see my family. I would do anything I had to do with a renewed strength as my home was in view.

The parable was told in the book of Matthew about the ten virgins; five were wise and five foolish. These virgins were all getting prepared to attend the wedding feast. Weddings always bring about excitement and happiness. I can just imagine the great care that was taken to be prepared for this special occasion. The virgins would have started preparing long before the wedding day. Garments would have to be sewn. The appropriate shoes would have to be sought for and bought.

The virgins were happy because the date of the wedding drew near. I can imagine that the garments were ready; they were washed and neatly pressed long before the date of the wedding.

The date arrived, and all of them had oil in their lamps waiting for the bridegroom. If the bridegroom had shown up at the time expected, everyone would have been welcomed in the marriage feast. But the bridegroom tarried, and all the virgins fell asleep. When the call came that the bridegroom had arrived, it was revealed then who was truly prepared and who was not. The wise virgins had extra oil for their lamps, the foolish ones did not. What would the foolish do? They were told to go seek as there was not sufficient to share. The virgins represent us who are living at the time of the end. The coming of the bridegroom drew near. Why didn't they have extra oil? Why were they not revived and reformed to meet the bridegroom?

As Christians, our lamps must always be trimmed and burning. We cannot afford to run out of oil while we are waiting for the Lord's return. He is almost at the door. We have to be constantly in prayer. We have to be reformed and rejuvenated each day. We have to continue having a revival.

What does the oil represent? It represents the Holy Spirit, who is our Comforter and our Guide. We must allow the Holy Spirit to guide us in our every move. When we are filled with the Holy Spirit, we will do things not according to our will but according to God's.

According to *The Coming of the Comforter*, by Leroy E. Froom, p. 103, the Holy Spirit convicts us of sin. He makes the hearers of the Word of God see themselves as God sees them. The indwelling of the Holy Spirit helps us to live holy lives.

Although Christ had given the promise to His disciples that they should receive the Holy Spirit, this did not remove the necessity of prayer. They prayed all the more earnestly; they continued in prayer with one accord (ibid., p. 93). This constant prayer kept their lamps burning, and their oil replenished.

The Holy Spirit is available today for us, but we must also be in constant prayer and supplication. The devil also speaks to us, but when we are in tune with God, we will know when the Holy Spirit is speaking to us and when the devil is speaking. Our oil cannot run dry as once we allow this to happen, our light will go out, and the prince of darkness will take control of our lives. God is not a God of darkness, and the Holy Spirit will not dwell in darkness.

The Lord is more willing to give the Holy Spirit to us than parents are to give good gifts to their children (ibid., p. 99).

The group of us had our revival shortly before we started the journey. Even though we started off very doubtful, Merlyn encouraged us, and by the end of the devotion, we were revived, ready to go home. This is the very same experience we must have each day. The group of us were revived, and we kept that spirit within us until we reached home. Our oils did not go out. It burned and burned until we reached home.

> **We are nearing home!**

On our Christian journey, now is the time for revival and reformation. We are nearing home! We must be engaged in serious soul searching. We cannot be looking for the faults in others. We have to seek them out in our own lives, and we must wrestle with our Father until all our sins are forgiven. We must wrestle just as how Jacob wrestled with Christ until he was blessed.

We must be engaged in serious prayer and fasting. Only then will we be able to overcome Satan's attacks.

Chapter 25

Keep Pressing On

The songwriter says, "I'm pressing on the upward way, new heights I'm gaining every day, still praying as I onward bound, Lord, plant my feet on higher ground." We purposed in our hearts that weekend that we were pressing on. We pressed on through all the difficulties that we faced. Some looked impossible, and we would not have been able to do it in our own strength. We pressed on when there was no path. We pressed on when faced with the huge rock with no apparent path. We pressed on most of the time silently but prayerfully.

We pressed on when we had to climb strings and rocks. We pressed on when we had to crawl on our bellies. We pressed on when we faced discouragements. We pressed on in the mountains. We pressed on when we got lost, and it seemed there was no way out. Yes, we kept pressing on the upward way, and new heights were gained every moment.

Does this sound familiar to our everyday life? Yes, it does! We go through struggles. When we are tempted, when we are tried, when we are tested, should we give up on our journey when we are almost in view of our heavenly home? A resounding NO!

The closer we are to home, the more Satan will heavily burden us down. What we need to do is press on. I have found a church sister who I have the privilege to call every day and pray together. We do not use the call to gossip, but we use the time to encourage each other and press on. I look forward to calling her each day, and after the prayer is finished on a daily basis, it leaves me with renewed strength. Sometimes it does not matter how low I feel before the prayer; at the end, it always leaves me with a mountain-top experience.

So, I continue to press on. My family continues to press on. When we face disappointments, we press on because we know what God has done for us in the past, and we know He will come through in the future.

The songwriter went on to say, "Lord, lift me up, and I shall stand by faith, on heaven's tableland; a higher plane than I have found, Lord, plant my feet on higher ground." I encourage those who are halting between two decisions to press on, looking for the truth. If you are sincere in your search, the Holy Spirit will lead you in the right path.

You might have never set foot into a church, but you want to find truth—press on. You might be a prostitute, and you want to change your lifestyle, so you are looking for Christ—press on.

Chapter 25: Keep Pressing On

You might be beaten down, and people might scorn you as they did Mary Magdalene—press on because God knows your heart, and He will help you find Him if you are sincere. You might have committed many crimes, you may have taken a life or many lives, the Lord can change you—so press on for truth.

The Lord is ready and able to save anyone who is willing to give Him their heart. To the utmost, Jesus saves! He will pick you up and turn you around. He is a compassionate God. It does not matter how deeply rooted you are in sin; it does not matter if others look down on you and believe that you are worth nothing. Give it all to Jesus, and He will make a way for you.

I want to scale the utmost height and catch a glimpse of glory bright. Yes, we want to have more than a glimpse of our heavenly home. We want to live in our heavenly home, so let us press on. Let us press on when we are humiliated because of our Christian faith, let us press on when we do not have a path to walk, let us press on when we cannot walk, let us press on when we only can crawl. Let us press on when we are lying in the bed of affliction because we know that soon and very soon, we are going to see our King.

- Press on through criticism
- Press on through ridicule
- Press on through skepticism
- Press on through scorn
- Press on when the way seems rocky and steep
- Press on when there is no way
- Press on through trials and tribulations
- Press on when we lose loved ones
- Press on when we are weak
- Press on when we are strong
- Press on when we are happy
- Press on when we are sad
- Press on through peer pressure
- Press on when we are on the mountain top
- Press on when we are low in the valley
- Press on when crossing deep, raging rivers
- Press on when it seems we have reached a point of no return

Home is where the heart is. When we were trying to cross the river to go home, our hearts were home. As a result of this, we did not feel the pain so much as we were struggling to go home. We gladly did whatever it took to reach home.

Our hearts should now be on our heavenly home. Let us purpose in our hearts to walk this Christian journey with Christ in our hearts. With Jesus, we can make it, and we know He will supply all our needs.

> Not as though I had already attained, either were already perfect: but I follow after, if that I may apprehend that for which also I am apprehended of Christ Jesus. Brethren, I count not myself to have apprehended: but this one thing I do, forgetting those things which are behind, and reaching forth unto those things which are before, I press toward the mark for the prize of the high calling of God in Christ Jesus. (Phil. 3:12–14)

Let us press on, press on, press on.

Chapter 26

Home at Last!

I could not believe it. I was home! Very soon, I was lying on my own bed and could turn at liberty. I did not have to listen out for "Turning Time." The rain fell, but I felt safe and warm. There is no place like home, and it's nice to be home after such a terrible ordeal. My Lord helped us to reach our homes safely. Praise be to God!

Christ is indeed coming back to gather His children and bring them home. Jesus, just before His crucifixion, said that He would go to prepare a place for us, and if He went, then He will return for us. Thanks be to God, He ascended into heaven, and the scripture says that He will return in like manner as the disciples saw Him go. At the first trump, those who die in the Lord will be raised incorruptible, and we will see Jesus, the One who has saved us from our sins. Those who are alive and remain shall be caught up to meet Him in the air, and so shall we ever be with the Lord (see 1 Thess. 4:17).

> *I could not believe it.*
> *I was home!*

The scripture says that we will remember the things of the earth no more. When we get to heaven, there will be joy forevermore. There will be no pain, no tears, no work to worry about being fired, no bank account to worry about losing our finances, no worrying about losing our houses because Jesus Himself has gone to prepare our homes. Praise the Lord, the banks will not be able to repossess them. There will be no bill collectors. We do not have to worry about the poisons in our food. We do not have to worry about the dangerous animals. As a matter of fact, the children will play with the lions and other animals that were once dangerous. We will see Jesus, the One who has saved us from sin and shame. The scripture says that we will go to heaven with Christ for a thousand years, after which the New Jerusalem will come down to earth and remain on earth. What a day that will be. Brothers and sisters, we have to make every effort to be a part of this world made new.

Home—where there will be no night because Jesus will be our light. Earth will be redeemed to its former beauty. Can you picture what this will look like? We will need no police department, no fire department. All these former things will be passed away.

Christ is in the Most Holy Place interceding for us, but soon and very soon, He will throw down His censer and will proclaim that it is finished. At His second coming, those who are righteous will remain righteous, and those who are filthy will remain filthy. It will be a time of joy for the righteous. The unrighteous will be calling out for the rocks and the mountains to fall on them because they will not be able to stand the brightness of Jesus Christ.

Chapter 26: Home at Last!

During our thousand years with the Lord, we will be reviewing the records of our brothers and sisters who did not make it to heaven. We will realize why such a member who was so active in the church did not make it. There will be surprises in heaven because people whom we believe will be there are going to be lost, and the ones whom we pushed aside and looked down on will make it to heaven.

Home at last! What joy it will bring to all those who make it to the kingdom. John said he saw a great number, both great and small. How happy we will be. Home! We are home! Home where there is no night. Home where there is no pain, no heartache or sickness, where we will be free to walk the streets of gold. We will sing the song of Moses and the Lamb. We will not be looking out for thieves and murderers. There will be peace forevermore. My brothers and sisters, let us keep the faith because we are almost home.

Revelation 1:7 says, "Behold, he cometh with clouds; and every eye shall see him, and they also which pierced him." Christ is coming again, and in Revelation 16:15, it says, "Behold, I come as a thief. Blessed is he that watcheth, and keepeth his garments, lest he walk naked, and they see his shame."

Christ will be coming like a thief in the night. We do not know when the thief will strike. If we knew, we would make every preparation and ensure that the thief is caught. We do not know when Christ will come, but just as we set up home securities, we can do the same by preparing to meet the coming Jesus. Revelation 22:7 says, "Behold, I come quickly: blessed is he that keepeth the sayings of the prophecy of this book."

Revelation 22:12, 14 says, "And, behold, I come quickly; and my reward is with me, to give to every man according as his work shall be. Blessed are they that do his commandments, that they may have right to the tree of life, and may enter in through the gates into the city."

John, in the book of Revelation, was on the isle of Patmos, and behold, the Lord God showed him the vision of the coming of Jesus Christ. And John said in Revelation 21:1–8,

And I saw a new heaven and a new earth: for the first heaven and the first earth were passed away; and there was no more sea. And I John saw the holy city, new Jerusalem, coming down from God out of heaven, prepared as a bride adorned for her husband. And I heard a great voice out of heaven saying, Behold, the tabernacle of God is with men, and he will dwell with them, and they shall be his people, and God himself shall be with them, and be their God. And God shall wipe away all tears from their eyes; and there shall be no more death, neither sorrow, nor crying, neither shall there be any more pain: for the former things are passed away. And he that sat upon the throne said, Behold, I make all things new. And he said unto me, Write: for these words are true and faithful."

John went on to describe the new city Jerusalem with walls of jasper stone, clear as crystal; the wall, great and high, twelve gates, and at the gates, twelve angels, and names written thereon, which are the names of the twelve tribes of the children of Israel. In Revelation 21:23, John said that "the city had no need of the sun, neither of the moon, to shine in it: for the glory of God did lighten it, and the Lamb is the light thereof."

Let us purpose in our hearts to serve God.

When we go to our heavenly home, we will sing songs the angels will not be able to sing. We will see Jesus, the One who died for our sins. Let us purpose in our hearts to serve God. Let us serve Him when it seems everything is against us. Let us serve Him when it seems our problems envelop us, and we do not even see or feel God in our trials. Let us serve Him in good times and in bad times because heaven will be worth it. I want to see my Jesus who died for me. I want to sit at His feet and learn more about Him. I want my friends to be there too. I want to be able to say, home at last!

Chapter 26: Home at Last!

When Jesus Comes

If you can picture the day the Lord will appear,
If you can envision when the clouds will roll back as a scroll,
When the Lord King of kings will take His children so dear,
Then you must be prepared and make it right with your soul.

Chorus
For when Jesus comes, O, I say, when Jesus comes
Will, will you be ready, when Jesus comes?
For the day is coming, and the day is sure.
O, my brother, be ready, when Jesus comes.

What a joy it will be to the faithful big and small,
Who through tribulation kept the faith, the faith of God.
Saints of God will be rejoicing they will be standing tall.
For the King He will come, and He will take their reward.

For when Jesus comes, O, I say, when Jesus comes,
O, my sister, be ready, when Jesus comes.

For when Jesus comes, O, I say, when Jesus comes,
Let us all be ready when Jesus comes.

By: Carline Samuels

Dear Jesus, please help me to be a witness to all I have come in contact with. Please help me to realize that I am just a pilgrim traveling through this world of sin. Help me to get ready and stay ready because Your redemption draws near. Help me not to get weary in doing good. Help me to continue to look to You for renewed strength each day. Help me not to only talk the talk but walk the walk. Help me to be a witness, a true witness for You.

Please send the Holy Spirit to attend to me minutely. I know I cannot do it by myself. Help me to submit to the Holy Spirit. Let Him have His way in my life. Please give me what to say and do each day because, without You, I can do absolutely nothing good.

Keep me near the cross, and help me that my oil will continue to burn brightly and will never go out. I want to make heaven my home. Lord, help me to do right. Help me to live each second as if it were the last second on earth. Give me the desire to study Your Word and to have a close relationship with You. I want to see You when You come. Not to be destroyed by the brightness of Your coming but to hear You say, "Welcome, thou good and faithful servant, enter into the joy of Your Lord." Just as I made it safely home from Halls Delight, help me to make it to my heavenly home.

Lord, until then, until You put in Your appearance, keep me safe, keep me close to You, keep me as the apple of Your eye, hide me behind the cross. Help me to get ready and stay ready to meet You at Your second coming.

Whatever I ask for myself, I ask for my husband, my children, my family, for Pastor Willis, Merlyn, Hirfa, and Veneice, my church family, friends, and whoever will read this book. Bless us, Lord, and save us in Your everlasting kingdom, I pray—

In Jesus Name.
Amen!

About the Author

Carline Verona Samuels is the fifth child of Vincent (deceased) and Evelyn Francis. She has four sisters—Bedel, Unet, Nathalie (deceased), and Aletha, and two brothers—Paul and Daniel. She is married to Holness, and the union has brought about four children—Kathrina, Shani, Kara, and Kevaun. She attended Brown's Town High School and Northern Caribbean University in Jamaica. Carline migrated to the United States from Jamaica in 2007 with her children to rejoin her husband. She earned a B.S. degree in organizational management (Summa Cum Laude) from Oakwood University in Huntsville, Alabama, and a master's in social work from Campbellsville University in Campbellsville, Kentucky. She has also received her licensure in social work. Carline loves to write, and she has penned more than 100 poems, songs, and a few skits. She believes that writing is a gift from God and is, therefore, making a concerted effort to use her talent more to the glory and honor of God. She prays that her inscription will touch as many lives as she possibly can so that lives may be changed and souls won for the kingdom of God.

She is a very sociable person and gets along amicably with people of varying temperaments. Her desire is for her and her family to go home with Jesus when He returns and is using this medium to witness to others so that they too may hear about God's goodness and make the decision to serve Him also.

References

Chapter 4
3 John 2

Chapter 5
James 4:7–8

Chapter 8
Ecclesiastes 9:10

Chapter 10
James 1:8
Isaiah 58:13–14
1 John 1:9

Chapter 12
Philippians 4:6–7
1 Corinthians 10:13

Chapter 13
White, Ellen G., *Selected Messages*, Book 2 (Washington, DC: Review and Herald Publishing Association, 1958), pp. 311–315.

Chapter 14
Psalm 37:25

Chapter 16
White, Ellen G., *Messages to Young People* (Hagerstown, MD: Review and Herald Publishing Association, 1930), p. 250.
James 5:16
Mark 11:22–23
Daniel 6
White, Ellen G., *Christ's Object Lessons* (Washington, DC: Review and Herald Publishing Association, 1900), p. 146.
"Prayer," *Daily Word* Magazine, Wednesday, June 18, 1952.

1 John 5:14–15
Hebrews 10:35
Chapter 17
Romans 8:38–39

Chapter 19
Psalm 23:4
Psalm 91:11–12
Matthew 24:13
Job 19:26–27
2 Timothy 2:11–12

Chapter 20
Brown, Walton J., *Angels: We Never Walk Alone*, 1st edition (Hagerstown, MD: Review and Herald Publishing Association, September 27, 1987), p. 58.
Psalm 19:11–12

Chapter 22
Matthew 5:10

Chapter 24
2 Peter 3:9–10
Matthew 5:44–45
Exodus 20:8–11
John 14:15
Hebrews 4:8–9
James 2:10–12
Genesis 1–2:1
Matthew 25:43

Chapter 25
Froom, Leroy E., *Coming of the Comforter*, Revised edition (Hagerstown, MD, Review and Herald Publishing Assn., January 1, 1956), p. 93, 103, 199.
Philippians 3:12–14

Chapter 26
    Revelation 1:7
    Revelation 16:15
    Revelation 22:7
    Revelation 22:12, 14
    Revelation 21:1–8
    Revelation 21:23

TEACH Services, Inc.
P U B L I S H I N G

We invite you to view the complete
selection of titles we publish at:
www.TEACHServices.com

We encourage you to write us
with your thoughts about this,
or any other book we publish at:
info@TEACHServices.com

TEACH Services' titles may be purchased in
bulk quantities for educational, fund-raising,
business, or promotional use.
bulksales@TEACHServices.com

Finally, if you are interested in seeing
your own book in print, please contact us at:
publishing@TEACHServices.com
We are happy to review your manuscript at no charge.

www.ingramcontent.com/pod-product-compliance
Lightning Source LLC
Chambersburg PA
CBHW071220160426
43196CB00012B/2359